TADEJ POGAČAR
BIOGRAPHY 2025

The Inspirational Story of His Journey from Slovenian Teen Sensation to One of the Most Complete Riders in Cycling History

John R. Hite

Copyright © 2025 by John R. Hite

TABLE OF CONTENTS

INTRODUCTION

It begins with a boy on a bike, climbing hills most adults would hesitate to walk. No spotlight, no crowd, just wheels crunching gravel and lungs burning with something far deeper than ambition. Before Tadej Pogačar became one of the most complete cyclists the sport has ever seen, before he pulled on the yellow jersey or stood on podiums with flags waving behind him, there was only a quiet Slovenian kid riding through wind and fog with a kind of joy that can't be taught. That joy would one day change cycling.

His story isn't a straight sprint to stardom. It's a winding ascent filled with surprises, heartbreaks, daring decisions, and moments of pure, unforgettable magic. For a sport rooted in tradition, where tactics are measured and progress is usually earned by inching forward year by year, Tadej tore through expectations like a rider cresting a summit with no one in his slipstream. From the moment he exploded onto the global stage, it was clear something had shifted. Here was a racer who defied categories: part climber, part tactician, part showman, and yet humble in a way that made his greatness feel approachable.

This book isn't just about races and results, though those matter. It's about a rare fusion of talent and temperament, about a mindset that embraces pressure but never becomes consumed by it. Readers will trace Tadej's steps from the dusty roads of Komenda to the grandest boulevards of Paris, from being a name whispered by insiders to a symbol of excellence known across continents. You'll relive the shock of his Tour de France debut, the fire of his rivalry with Jonas Vingegaard, the thrill of his mountain raids, and the grace with which he handled defeat. You'll see how he carved victories not just from strength but from moments when others hesitated and he did not.

What makes his journey so captivating is the way it blends power with unpredictability. Tadej doesn't follow cycling's conventional script. He writes his own chapters, attacking when logic says wait, smiling when the pain sets in, laughing off setbacks and always, somehow, coming back stronger. His audacity reawakened something in the sport: a sense of wonder, a reminder that racing is also an art form. His story has made cycling more human again.

But this is more than a tale of triumphs. It's a portrait of someone who, despite unimaginable success, remains grounded by the same passion that first pulled him toward two wheels. A competitor with nerves of steel and the heart of a dreamer. A global icon who still jokes with fans, still finds comfort in forests and solitude, and still rides as if chasing something far bigger than medals.

Tadej Pogačar's rise is not a coincidence. It's a masterclass in courage, patience, and raw, unfiltered love for the ride. Whether you're a lifelong cycling devotee or a newcomer looking to understand what makes greatness feel effortless, this is the story of a young man who changed the sport, not with noise, but with clarity of purpose.

Welcome to the world of Tadej. It doesn't follow the map. But the view from here is unforgettable.

Chapter 1
From Klanec to Global Dreams

How a quiet Slovenian village shaped a boy who refused to ride within limits

In the rolling green hills of Slovenia, tucked just northwest of Ljubljana, sits the unassuming village of Klanec near Komenda. A place where life moves slowly, where neighbors still wave from porches, and where cows outnumber cars. It's the kind of village most people might pass through without a second thought. But for Tadej Pogačar, it was the launchpad for a journey that would one day ripple through the world of professional cycling like a lightning strike across calm skies.

Tadej was not born into wealth, nor was he immediately surrounded by elite athletic infrastructure. What he did have was space, endless space to ride, explore, fall, get up, and ride some more. His earliest memories weren't shaped in velodromes or on manicured tracks. They were carved into the rough, uneven country roads of Klanec, where gravel crackled under his tires and each curve offered a new adventure. Before he could fully grasp what cycling was, Tadej understood what freedom felt like, wind on his face, legs pumping, heart soaring. That feeling would stay with him long after his hometown was left behind in his rearview mirror.

His parents, Mirko and Marjeta, were supportive but practical. Neither pushed him into sport, but neither tried to hold him back. His mother worked in a textile factory and his father was involved in the administration of Komenda's local municipality. They were hardworking people with modest means, and their values ran deep. There was no room for arrogance in the Pogačar household, no tolerance for shortcuts. Tadej grew up not knowing that other kids elsewhere were spending hours in cycling academies. He was content making laps around the village, pushing a rusty old bike to its limits, challenging himself to ride faster, longer, and steeper.

What started as play soon turned into something else. By the time he was nine, people in the village began to notice the boy who didn't stop pedaling. He didn't talk much about dreams or victories, he just rode. There was a quiet determination in him, the kind that wasn't loud but impossible to ignore. While others lost interest, distracted by television, video games, or team sports, Tadej kept returning to his bike. When his first real race came, a small local event for children, he pedaled like he had something to prove, not to others, but to himself.

And that's what separated him, even then. It wasn't medals that drove him. It was the need to feel the road beneath him, to push until his lungs burned and his vision narrowed. There was no crowd cheering him from the sidelines on those long rides between cornfields and forests. No social media followers or global fans. Just a boy chasing a feeling. That chase soon led him to KD Rog, a local cycling club in Ljubljana known for nurturing young talent. But even at the club, surrounded by kids from more competitive backgrounds, Tadej stood out, not because he was the strongest, but because he treated each training session like it was sacred.

At KD Rog, the coaches noticed the boy from Komenda was different. He wasn't flashy, didn't show off, didn't speak much unless spoken to. But when he climbed, something changed. His legs moved with a rhythm that felt natural, almost melodic. And while others groaned at the thought of hill repeats or endurance rides in the rain, Tadej welcomed it. Suffering didn't deter him. It was something he embraced, quietly, almost gratefully. His body language didn't scream for attention, but the stopwatch never lied.

Back home in Klanec, he still did his chores, still stayed close to family. He was the same soft-spoken boy who helped his parents in the garden and played soccer with his older brother Tilen in the backyard. Fame hadn't touched him, nor had ambition twisted his innocence. Yet those close to him began to realize that this wasn't just a phase. Cycling wasn't a hobby to Tadej, it was his language, his outlet, his future waiting patiently on the horizon.

The hills around Klanec became his first battleground. He memorized the gradients, timed himself up the climbs, imagined what it would be like to attack them in a race scenario. He didn't need a coach to teach him how to visualize victory; he did it instinctively. Often, he would wave goodbye to his family in the morning and return home hours later, sweat-soaked, legs trembling, eyes glowing. No one forced him to ride that long or that hard. He was simply built that way, to test limits, to ride until the line between effort and joy blurred into something only he could understand.

And yet, despite his growing prowess, he never lost the gentle humility that defined him. When he started gaining attention on the junior circuit, when he began winning regional titles, he still returned to his village the same way: quietly, without ceremony. Neighbors who had seen him ride past their homes as a boy now began following his name in cycling bulletins and online forums. But he never distanced himself from them. Even as the wins piled up, Tadej's sense of place, his roots in the narrow, sun-dappled streets of Klanec, only grew stronger.

There is something profound about an elite athlete who never forgets where it all began. For Pogačar, every major triumph would forever

5

be linked to those first solo rides through fields and farm roads, those early days when the only sound was the wind, his breath, and the hum of wheels on tarmac. It shaped him not just physically, but spiritually. He didn't just learn to ride in Klanec, he learned to listen to his body, to trust silence, to work when no one was watching, and to believe that greatness begins with small, consistent acts of courage.

Years later, as he stood atop podiums in Paris, Milan, and Rome, reporters would ask him about his tactics, his rivals, his ambitions. But every now and then, someone would ask what got him into cycling in the first place. He'd smile and talk about the village where it all began, the old bike with clunky gears, the endless roads with no destination but motion itself.

Those early rides through Klanec were not just the start of a career, they were the foundation of a mindset. A mindset that told him there were no limits, just new distances to cover. A mindset that carried him from the whispering hills of Slovenia to the thunderous roars of cycling's grandest stages. And through it all, that small town, with its quiet roads and wide skies, remained the one place where a young boy learned to dream without boundaries. Not through words. Through pedals.

The role of Tilen Pogačar in igniting the spark that would become a global fire

Before the cycling world ever knew the name Tadej Pogačar, before yellow jerseys and solo climbs turned him into a modern legend, there was another Pogačar pedaling with purpose. His name was Tilen, Tadej's older brother, and he was the first to feel the pull of the open road, the first to fall in love with the rhythm of riding. Long before Tadej realized what cycling could be, it was Tilen who brought that world into their home, filling it with wheels, gears, race stories, and dreams that quietly lit a fuse in his younger sibling's heart.

Growing up in the small Slovenian village of Klanec near Komenda, Tilen was the pioneer in a family that had no real tradition in competitive cycling. Their parents, Mirko and Marjeta, encouraged activity but didn't push their boys toward medals or trophies. Tilen, always curious and slightly restless, gravitated toward bikes on his own terms. As a young teenager, he joined KD Rog, one of Slovenia's most respected cycling clubs. He wasn't chasing glory; he was looking for belonging, for a way to test himself that went beyond schoolbooks and small-town expectations.

When Tilen started training seriously, the family dynamic began to shift in subtle but powerful ways. The living room TV began showing race highlights instead of cartoons. Conversations at dinner gradually tilted toward gradients, gear ratios, and upcoming competitions. And Tadej, still just a boy trying to keep up, watched all of this unfold with wide eyes. His brother's commitment, the intensity with which he spoke about riding, the glow of excitement after training sessions, it was magnetic. Tadej didn't have to be told to fall in love with cycling; he simply watched his brother and followed instinctively.

Their bond wasn't marked by loud declarations or dramatic moments. It was quiet and consistent. When Tilen came home from rides, Tadej would pepper him with questions: How fast did you go? What did the climb feel like? Who was the strongest in the group? Tilen answered everything with the patience of someone who knew he was shaping more than just a conversation. He was handing down a passion, one pedal stroke at a time.

Sometimes, Tilen would let Tadej tag along on his warm-up rides, even though the younger boy's legs couldn't possibly keep up. They'd ride through the same narrow backroads, the wind pulling at their jerseys, the sun cutting through the trees, and in those moments, it wasn't about who was faster. It was about sharing something sacred, a language built without words. Tadej absorbed everything: the posture, the pacing, the rituals. He noticed how Tilen checked tire pressure before every ride, how he timed his hydration, how he respected the bike as more than a machine. These small lessons became habits long before Tadej knew they were shaping his future.

As Tilen progressed in his training, he began racing more seriously in Slovenia's competitive youth scene. His results were respectable, and he earned admiration within the local cycling community. But more importantly, he carried the flag for the Pogačar family, proving that cycling wasn't just a phase or a fantasy. It was real. It was achievable. When he raced in regional competitions, Tadej was often on the sidelines, cheering with quiet intensity, watching not just as a fan but as a student.

Though they were brothers, Tilen never saw Tadej as competition. He saw potential, raw, explosive, and full of wonder. Tilen recognized that his younger brother had something different, something less taught and more innate. It wasn't just talent; it was a kind of intuitive feel for the road, a deep connection with the motion of cycling that couldn't be manufactured. Instead of letting ego interfere, Tilen became Tadej's earliest supporter, encouraging him to train, to join KD Rog, to start racing, even when Tadej didn't yet believe he belonged.

There were moments when Tadej doubted himself. He was naturally introverted, uncomfortable with attention, and unsure whether he could really turn his love for the sport into something meaningful. But Tilen never wavered. He offered quiet validation, a ride shared, a compliment given when it mattered most, a bike part borrowed with a knowing smile. His belief wasn't loud or theatrical. It was steady. And for a shy boy trying to find his voice through pedals and climbs, that belief was everything.

As Tadej's rise began, first slowly, then rapidly, Tilen's role began to shift. He was no longer just the older brother; he became a sounding board, a confidant, and at times, a grounding force. When journalists and fans started to take notice of Tadej's performances, it was Tilen who reminded him of why he started riding in the first place. Not for cameras. Not for fame. But for the simple love of motion, for the thrill of a ride through the hills of Klanec, for the bond they'd built long before trophies entered the picture.

Tilen also played a subtle yet critical role in helping Tadej manage early expectations. With experience in cycling's local circuit, he understood the pressures of racing, the politics of team selection, the emotional rollercoaster of form and fatigue. He offered guidance without preaching, always letting Tadej carve his own path. But his presence, unwavering and humble, gave Tadej the stability to chase something bigger without losing touch with who he was.

As the years passed and Tadej's star rose beyond what even the proudest brother could have predicted, Tilen remained close, not in the spotlight, but never far from it. When Tadej won the Tour de France for the first time, he spoke not just about coaches and teammates, but about the boy who first showed him how to clip into pedals, the brother who pedaled hard long before anyone else was watching.

Tilen's story is rarely told in cycling broadcasts or Tour documentaries. Yet his fingerprint is etched into every stage win, every mountain breakaway, every attack that left seasoned veterans stunned. Without Tilen, there might not have been a Tadej as we know him. Not because Tilen made his brother great, but because he helped him believe that greatness was worth pursuing. He showed him that joy and discipline could coexist, that family could fuel ambition, and that love for a sport could be passed down like a cherished family tradition.

The story of Tadej Pogačar cannot be fully understood without the quiet sacrifices and relentless belief of his older brother. Tilen rode so his little brother could dream. And when that dream grew into something unimaginable, he was there, not leading the way anymore, but walking beside it, proud, steady, and still believing.

Meeting the mentor who turned potential into purpose at the Rog Cycling Club

When Tadej Pogačar first rolled through the gates of KD Rog Cycling Club in Ljubljana, he didn't look like the future of the sport. He was skinny, quiet, and not particularly commanding in appearance. His bike, by the standards of many young prospects, was modest. There were no flashy decals, no carbon wheels humming like jet engines. What stood out, though, even on that first day, wasn't what he had, but how he moved. A coach standing at the edge of the training lot watched him weave between cones and thought, there's something different about this kid. That coach was Andrcj Hauptman, a former Olympian and Slovenian national icon who would become the mentor Tadej didn't know he needed, and the architect of a transformation that would shake the cycling world.

At the time, Hauptman wasn't just coaching at KD Rog, he was building a system. A pathway. He knew from his own experience the grind, isolation, and emotional volatility that came with trying to become a world-class cyclist from a small Central European nation. Slovenia didn't have the deep-rooted cycling culture of France or Italy, nor the industrial scouting systems of Belgium or the Netherlands. What it did have was raw, unshaped talent. Hauptman's mission was to spot it early and shape it right. When he saw Tadej, he didn't just see a boy who could ride fast, he saw a rider with no ceiling.

Tadej was 9 when he first entered the junior ranks of KD Rog, but his formal connection with Hauptman would solidify a few years later when the boy had developed enough power, maturity, and curiosity to start drawing serious coaching attention. By then, his commitment was obvious, not in loud declarations or wild ambitions, but in the way he never missed training, how he pedaled with discipline even when no one was looking, and how he never once complained, no matter the weather, distance, or fatigue. He was that rare mix of humility and hunger, and Hauptman, who had once been a teenage prodigy himself, recognized the fire.

Their first real conversations weren't about strategy or power output. They were about mindset. Hauptman asked Tadej why he rode. Not what he wanted to win. Not who he wanted to beat. But why. It was a probing question, the kind that stopped Tadej in his tracks. The boy didn't answer immediately, because he never thought of it that way. He only knew that cycling made him feel alive, like he had purpose, direction, and space to be fully himself. That was all Hauptman needed to hear. Purpose was something a coach could build on. Talent was common. Purpose was sacred.

The structure of their relationship evolved naturally. Hauptman didn't hover or dominate, he observed, nudged, challenged. He gave Tadej hard tasks and watched how he responded. When others flinched, Pogačar leaned in. If training ended at 5 p.m., he'd stay until 5:30 to practice a weak corner. If intervals called for five repetitions, he'd sometimes do six. Not to impress anyone, simply because it didn't feel finished. That obsessive attention to completion, to the invisible edge, convinced Hauptman that this wasn't just a junior rider with a bright future. This was someone who could redefine what was possible.

Hauptman started tailoring training specifically to Pogačar's unique traits. He noticed early on that Tadej had an unusual capacity to recover, not just physically, but mentally. After a hard stage or interval set, most juniors would walk around dazed, needing downtime and motivation. Tadej would bounce back with a calm smile and ask, "What's next?" This trait would later become one of his superpowers in stage racing, his ability to ride consecutive brutal mountain stages with consistency was rooted in those early days of youth training.

They worked on more than just numbers. Hauptman taught Pogačar how to read races, not just ride them. They watched tapes together, studied attacks, analyzed riders' body language. He showed him how to conserve energy in the peloton, when to surge on a climb, when to bluff and when to strike. But he also talked about what it meant to be a complete cyclist: how to handle interviews, respect rivals, lead with humility, and inspire teammates. There was no shortcut to greatness, Hauptman would say. It wasn't about talent alone. It was about showing up differently than the rest, every single day.

Their relationship deepened during international trips, where Tadej began competing against stronger fields. These were the first real tests, not just of fitness, but of belief. It was one thing to dominate local circuits. It was another to line up against Dutch, French, and Italian riders raised in cycling schools, riding bikes that cost more than the Pogačars' family car. Hauptman shielded Tadej from the noise and gave him one simple instruction: "You belong here." He repeated it before every major race, every intimidating starting line. "You belong here." It wasn't a pep talk. It was a reprogramming.

What truly set Hauptman apart as a mentor was that he never coached Pogačar to be a winner. He coached him to be free, free to attack when others wouldn't, to ride with joy and intuition, to trust the sensation in his legs over the data on his screen. He believed in balance, in allowing the human part of the rider to breathe. Even when they introduced power meters and more advanced metrics, he warned Tadej not to lose the feeling. "The numbers are tools," he'd say. "But you ride with your soul."

As Pogačar advanced into the under-23 ranks, the dynamic between them shifted again, now from teacher-student to something more like co-pilots. Hauptman never treated him like a child prodigy to be protected. He treated him like a man who needed to make his own decisions, sometimes even his own mistakes. When other coaches might have pulled back on expectations to protect a young star, Hauptman kept raising the bar. Not because he was ruthless, because he knew Tadej was capable of surprising even himself.

Their final years together at KD Rog were bittersweet. The writing was on the wall: Tadej was going places no Slovenian cyclist had ever gone before, not even Hauptman. When UAE Team Emirates came calling, when the big contract offers started to surface, Hauptman didn't stand in the way. He helped Tadej navigate the negotiations, the agents, the logistics, all while reminding him of the kid who first rode through the club gates on a quiet afternoon, just looking for somewhere to ride.

Even after Pogačar left the club system, their connection never truly ended. Hauptman would continue to offer advice behind the scenes, and Pogačar, now in the spotlight, never forgot to mention his mentor in interviews, on victory podiums, and even during setbacks. When asked who understood him best as a rider, his answer was always the same: "Coach Hauptman." Because it wasn't just coaching. It was transformation, the kind that reaches deeper than quads and VO2 max, the kind that begins with belief and ends with legacy.

What made their bond powerful was never a single victory or moment. It was the accumulation of years, of rain-soaked intervals, of hard truths exchanged in vans and hotel hallways, of a boy growing into a man under the gaze of someone who saw the full picture long before anyone else. Coach Pog had met Coach Pogi, and together, they'd turned potential into purpose, and purpose into a revolution on two wheels.

Chapter 2
The Prodigy No One Saw Coming

The 2018 race that made insiders whisper: "This kid might win the Tour someday"

In the summer of 2018, a quiet storm gathered in the French Alps, and only a few truly noticed its power. The Tour de l'Avenir, often called the "Tour de France for under-23 riders", is a proving ground that doesn't usually draw global attention. But for those who follow the sport with a keen eye, it's a crystal ball. This is where legends give their first serious hint, where the raw outlines of future champions sharpen just enough to make the faithful whisper, "Watch this one." That August, Tadej Pogačar arrived in France not as a headline, but as a curiosity, a wiry Slovenian with a shy smile and the kind of legs that, according to insiders, might be hiding something rare.

No one had him circled as the favorite. He wasn't even the biggest name in his own Slovenian squad. The spotlight tilted toward Bjorg Lambrecht of Belgium, Gino Mäder of Switzerland, and a handful of other polished young contenders already on WorldTour radars. Pogačar had quietly impressed at smaller races, but to the larger cycling world, he was still largely an unknown, a second-tier threat, perhaps capable of a good result, but not expected to shake the foundations of the race.

His early stages were steady, unspectacular, deliberately so. He rode smart, stayed hidden in the peloton, avoided unnecessary risks. Observers mistook his restraint for limitation. What they missed was calculation. Pogačar was measuring the field, learning the rhythms of the race, feeling for the cracks in the armor of those ahead of him. The opening stages didn't require his fire, they required patience, a skill most 19-year-olds haven't yet mastered. But Tadej was never a typical teenager, and he didn't come to France to impress anyone with a flashy breakaway. He came to win.

The Tour de l'Avenir has long been a battleground shaped by altitude. The race is known for saving its most brutal mountain stages for the final days, where raw talent alone means little. Riders are exposed not only to gradients that challenge the lungs but to the psychological toll of five-hour days on paper-thin roads surrounded by the ghosts of past champions. On Stage 7, everything changed. The race shifted upward, into the peaks, into the pain, and Tadej emerged from the mist like he had been waiting for this terrain all along.

That stage was a turning point, not because he took the lead yet, but because of how he rode when others cracked. The peloton splintered on the final climb, elite riders were shelled out the back, and Pogačar, expressionless, stayed glued to the front group. There was no grimace, no panicked breathing, just rhythm, relentless and composed. Coaches began exchanging glances in the team cars. Commentators dug into their notes, scrambling to say something meaningful about the Slovenian whose numbers had never screamed prodigy. What they saw now was undeniable.

Stage 8 confirmed it. It was mountainous, chaotic, and emotionally charged, the kind of day when legs aren't enough. As rivals launched attacks, Tadej never chased with desperation. He timed every effort like a surgeon with a scalpel, cutting seconds when they mattered most. With every pedal stroke, he was rewriting the narrative. He crossed the line not first, but where he needed to be. His name moved to the top of the general classification, and suddenly, the race belonged to him.

Journalists began to whisper, then write. "Who is this Pogačar?" Analysts looked at the splits and tried to make sense of the numbers. He wasn't dominating with brute force. He was winning with intelligence, timing, and an invisible engine that seemed to grow stronger as others faded. His climbing style wasn't violent, it was liquid. Where others bobbed and rocked, he stayed still. When he attacked, it wasn't to show strength; it was to exploit the exact moment someone else faltered. His instinct wasn't to follow, it was to lead with calm, with faith in his sensations. It didn't matter if others had better sprint numbers or climbing résumés. He understood the race on a level that belied his age.

By Stage 9, Pogačar was not just wearing the leader's jersey, he was transforming it into prophecy. That stage, which finished atop the Col de la Loze, tested every metric of a young rider's promise: endurance, tactics, fearlessness. As the gradient steepened, he launched a solo effort not out of arrogance but out of clarity. He sensed the moment. His team's support had been tight all week, but in the final five kilometers, it was Tadej alone, rising into the sky while others ground into survival mode. He didn't crush them. He floated away.

When he crossed the line that day, Tour scouts and team directors weren't just taking notes, they were calling agents. What they had seen wasn't just a victory. It was a blueprint. He didn't win the Tour de l'Avenir by overpowering the field. He won it by seeing what others couldn't, gaps in momentum, slivers of opportunity, and most of all, belief in his own process. By the time the final stage wrapped and he was crowned champion, it wasn't just his team smiling. The cycling world had seen enough to feel something more than admiration. They felt anticipation.

What made his win different wasn't just the margin, though it was significant. It was how he never looked like he was fighting the race. It was as if he had already studied the script. Other winners of the Tour de l'Avenir had passed through this gate: Egan Bernal, Miguel Ángel López, Nairo Quintana. But Pogačar's performance had a softness around the edges that made it unsettling. He didn't ride like someone trying to prove a point. He rode like someone who knew he belonged at the next level, and simply let the result arrive on schedule.

After the final podium ceremony, tucked away from the cameras, a handful of WorldTour coaches gathered for a quiet drink in the parking lot of a nearby café. One of them, a veteran talent scout from a French team, leaned back in his chair and said something that no one contradicted: "If this kid doesn't win the Tour someday, I'll eat my credentials." It was said half in jest, half in awe. Because what they had witnessed wasn't luck, or form, or a hot week in the mountains. It was foreshadowing.

The Tour de l'Avenir didn't just introduce Tadej Pogačar to the world. It introduced the idea that cycling's future might not follow the old rules. That dominance could be quiet. That greatness might come not in explosive moments but in the elegant threading of dozens of smaller ones. And that somewhere between youth and stardom, a 19-year-old from Slovenia had seen something that everyone else missed, the full picture, waiting to be painted.

Why a bold decision at age 20 changed the fate of a team, and a sport

When Tadej Pogačar signed with UAE Team Emirates in July 2018, he was just 19 years old, virtually unknown outside of niche cycling circles, and still soaking in the afterglow of his stunning win at the Tour de l'Avenir. The cycling world had just begun whispering his name, yet to many insiders, his next move would be the true test of how serious his trajectory might become. Where most young riders of his profile would look to established European teams with a history of developing Tour champions, Movistar, Jumbo-Visma, or Ineos, Tadej made a decision that stunned observers and quietly shifted the tectonic plates beneath the sport's elite structures. He didn't just pick a team. He picked a challenge, a project, and a belief system. UAE Team Emirates wasn't yet considered a superpower in 2018. But it was about to become one. And Tadej Pogačar would be the reason why.

When the deal was announced, the headlines didn't explode. The transfer wasn't treated like a revolution, nor was the team immediately flooded with fanfare. But behind the scenes, cycling's top talent scouts felt the ripple. Mauro Gianetti, the general manager of UAE Team Emirates, had moved decisively. He saw something others hadn't fully processed yet, something in the way Tadej handled pressure, in how he measured his efforts, in his maturity off the bike. Gianetti wasn't looking for the next solid stage racer. He was betting on a generational rider. And he was ready to build an empire around him.

For Tadej, the decision wasn't rooted in glamour. The team didn't yet have the historical pull of a Movistar or the scientific might of Team Sky. What they had was belief. Direct contact. Clarity. UAE's leadership didn't just throw numbers at him. They told him he would

19

be treated not as a development rider, but as a co-architect of something ambitious. They didn't want to fold him into a rigid system of incremental growth. They wanted to let him ride like himself. That freedom, that trust, was irresistible to a rider who had always moved by instinct.

He consulted his mentor Andrej Hauptman, who would eventually join the UAE setup himself. Hauptman understood what Pogačar needed, not just a race calendar, but a space to breathe. Some teams had expressed interest but were more cautious, more traditional. They spoke about long-term progression, perhaps looking at 2022 or 2023 as realistic years to bring him into the Grand Tour conversation. UAE Team Emirates spoke differently. They didn't ask him to wait. They asked him what he saw when he closed his eyes. Tadej told them he wanted to ride the Tour de France one day. They didn't laugh. They said, "Let's get ready."

The infrastructure around Pogačar began to shift rapidly. The team invested not only in his race preparation but also in his psychological and nutritional development. They knew raw numbers wouldn't be enough. They needed to keep him protected, not from rivals, but from the noise. He was still a teenager, newly exposed to the pressure cooker of WorldTour cycling. The team's approach was surgical. They gave him room to settle into the professional ranks without being immediately thrust into the limelight. Instead of overwhelming him with expectations, they focused on giving him the tools to make his own decisions. That was their masterstroke, treating him not like a kid with promise, but like a man with a plan.

His first race for UAE in early 2019, the Volta ao Algarve, didn't take long to validate the risk. Pogačar won a stage and finished overall winner of the race. He showed poise on climbs, delivered powerful time trials, and responded to surges from older riders with eerie calm. The cycling press began paying closer attention. What had seemed like a clever signing now looked like something more. In every interview, he was humble, grounded, often soft-spoken. But under the surface, it was clear he wasn't just thrilled to be in the big leagues, he was already thinking like a leader.

Throughout that debut season, the young Slovenian proved that his L'Avenir success was not a fluke. He finished third in the Tour of California. Then came his breakthrough Grand Tour debut, the 2019 Vuelta a España. No one expected a podium. His presence in the race was considered an investment in experience. Instead, he won three mountain stages and finished third overall, shocking everyone, including his rivals. He attacked when others sat still. He dropped riders with pedigrees and double his experience. He made calculated chaos seem effortless.

That Vuelta changed the conversation. Tadej Pogačar wasn't just a project anymore. He was a force. And UAE Team Emirates? No longer a middleweight. Their bold choice had paid off in full view of the cycling world. The spotlight shifted, and the team's credibility surged. Sponsors came knocking. Riders who once would've dismissed the team as a transitional stop began circling. They didn't just want to ride for UAE, they wanted to ride with Pogačar. The balance of power was shifting, and it began with a teenager's signature on a contract no one had expected.

Pogačar's loyalty didn't waver. As offers poured in, he remained anchored to the project that had believed in him from day one. He extended his contract multiple times, each time doubling down on his belief in the system being built around him. He wasn't just racing for himself, he was helping mold a new identity for a team now obsessed with detail, culture, and long-term excellence. He welcomed teammates with warmth and no ego, but his performances left no doubt about who was driving the ship.

What made the partnership so extraordinary wasn't just the mutual success. It was how both parties evolved together. Pogačar matured into a complete rider, taking lessons from his coaches, nutritionists, and older teammates, blending his natural instincts with a sharpened tactical brain. Meanwhile, UAE Team Emirates reinvented itself, investing heavily in data analytics, recruiting world-class climbers and domestiques, and committing to Tour de France campaigns that had real substance.

When the pandemic-affected 2020 Tour de France rolled around, UAE's gamble would crystallize into something legendary. Pogačar, still just 21, was not even the designated team leader at the start. But stage by stage, he climbed into contention. And on the penultimate stage, in one of the most surreal time trials in Tour history, he overtook his countryman Primož Roglič and won the yellow jersey. The world watched a 21-year-old redefine destiny in real time. From unsigned teenager to Tour champion in less than two years, all under the UAE Team Emirates banner.

That moment wasn't the finish line of their story. It was ignition. The team doubled down, supporting him with deeper rosters, more technology, and trust that never wavered. And Tadej, still disarmingly modest, never lost touch with the soul of the decision that brought him there: a belief that he could be more than just another name in a peloton if given the space to lead, fail, grow, and inspire.

At age 20, Tadej Pogačar didn't just make a career move. He ignited a movement. And by choosing UAE Team Emirates, he didn't just join a team, he transformed one. The sport, often slow to change and built on tradition, had been given a new blueprint: talent fused with vision, youth paired with freedom, belief matched by boldness. And it all began with one contract, quietly signed by a boy who already rode like he knew the future was his to shape.

His debut in 2019 and the jaw-dropping Vuelta performance that sent shockwaves across Europe

The 2019 Vuelta a España wasn't supposed to be a stage for history. The big stories had already been written in whispers before the race began: Primož Roglič, the Slovenian dynamo from Jumbo-Visma, was aiming for his first Grand Tour title. Alejandro Valverde was expected to be dangerous, again. Miguel Ángel López looked ready to pounce. The race was stacked with veterans and tacticians. Quietly, among the many names printed on start lists and preview articles, a 20-year-old debutant from UAE Team Emirates appeared. Few mentioned him as a threat. Some barely noticed him. His name was Tadej Pogačar.

He had only turned professional earlier that year. There were sparks already, victories in the Volta ao Algarve, an overall podium at the Tour of California, but a Grand Tour is different. It isn't just about talent. It's about survival. It's about enduring twenty-one days across mountains, flats, wind-swept cross-sections, and the constant psychological strain of defending, attacking, or watching everything slip away. It wasn't expected that a kid barely old enough to rent a car in most countries could handle that pressure. The Vuelta would be a learning opportunity, a stretch of the legs, a test. What happened instead was one of the most extraordinary three-week performances by a Grand Tour debutant in modern cycling history.

From the opening days, he rode without fear. Not recklessly, not wildly, but with a conviction that startled seasoned watchers. He placed himself well in the peloton, stayed alert, and conserved energy when required. His first few stages didn't scream promise. He was there, safely, somewhere in the group. But there were no mistakes. No signs of stress. His team didn't rush him. They protected him when needed, let him feel the rhythm of the race, and waited to see how his legs would respond when the terrain began to rise.

The mountains arrived early enough. Stage 9 to Cortals d'Encamp in Andorra was brutal, a high-altitude gauntlet with unpredictable weather and steep, punishing climbs. It was the kind of day where Grand Tour legs either show up or fall apart. And as the mist settled over the Pyrenees and chaos unfolded on the road, Tadej Pogačar made his move. Not a tentative surge. Not an opportunistic wheel-surf. A bold, defining attack. And he didn't just go. He dropped his rivals, one by one, in the thinnest air of the race so far. The boy from Komenda crossed the line first. He won the stage. He made people sit up. And with that one ride, the Vuelta had a new storyline, whether anyone was ready for it or not.

Reporters scrambled. Profiles were updated. Who was this teenager who had just taken a summit finish in a Grand Tour against established contenders? Coaches and former pros began combing through old footage, searching for hints they might have missed. The calmness. The positioning. The way he never looked rushed. They saw it now. And they knew this wasn't a fluke.

Pogačar's performance in the days that followed wasn't about one big explosion. It was about consistency, resilience, and a razor-sharp understanding of his own body. He never overexerted. He never cracked. On every mountain stage, he delivered. On every descent,

24

he stayed upright and composed. On every flat stage, he found safety in the peloton. It was a textbook masterclass from a rider barely old enough to remember the days of Armstrong and Contador with any true clarity.

Then came Stage 13, the mythical Los Machucos climb. A beast of a finish, famous for its double-digit gradients and soul-crushing ramps. That day was expected to shake the GC into pieces. Many figured Pogačar might begin to show the weight of accumulated fatigue. Instead, he held his own with clinical pacing. He didn't win the stage, but he stayed glued to the main contenders and limited any losses to seconds, not minutes. It was one of those rides that made experienced cycling fans murmur, "That kid is for real."

But it was Stage 20 that turned whispers into roars.

He wasn't the GC leader. He wasn't the one tasked with defending red. He was still technically riding as a support act to more seasoned UAE riders. But on the penultimate day, with the Vuelta deep into Asturias' mountains and riders bleeding time across every corner of the profile, Pogačar launched the kind of assault that gets replayed for decades. With 39 kilometers remaining, an eternity by Grand Tour standards, he attacked on the climb to Puerto de Peña Negra. It wasn't a burst. It was a breakaway for the ages.

And then, against every textbook rule, he never looked back.

For over an hour, he rode solo through mountain roads with a face of complete serenity. Not anguish. Not panic. Just flow. The peloton behind splintered. Top-10 riders tried to follow and failed. Analysts kept refreshing their screens, not believing what they saw. With every kilometer, he took back time on those ahead of him. And by the time he crossed the line in Plataforma de Gredos, arms raised and mouth barely open in celebration, he had claimed his third stage win of the Vuelta, and vaulted himself onto the final podium in Madrid.

He finished third overall. He was twenty years old. No one had done anything like it in a generation. Not even the sport's greatest climbers, Froome, Nibali, Quintana, had started their Grand Tour résumés this way. Pogačar hadn't just survived. He had transformed the race. He took the white jersey for best young rider, but it was clear to everyone watching that what he'd earned was something more intangible: fear from his rivals, and awe from the cycling world.

The media wanted stories. But Tadej wasn't feeding them hyperbole. His interviews were modest. He credited his team, said he was just trying to "do his job." But those who watched closely saw something else. They saw the beginning of a reign. He wasn't just fast. He was emotionally impervious to the rollercoaster of a Grand Tour. The stress didn't touch him. The attention didn't sway him. He rode like a ghost through the peloton, present, but untouchable.

That 2019 Vuelta became a moment frozen in cycling's collective memory, not because a young rider did something impressive, but because something inside the sport shifted. It had always been assumed that experience, years of learning, and careful guidance were prerequisites to a Grand Tour podium. Pogačar shattered that assumption. He didn't wait for permission to climb the ladder. He scaled it, two rungs at a time, without flinching.

By the time the Vuelta caravan rolled into Madrid and the cameras clicked bchind champagne glasses and final jersey presentations, everyone knew his name. He didn't just arrive. He arrived like a thunderclap. The youngest rider on the final podium had ridden the most mature race. And though he didn't wear red, it was clear who had stolen the soul of the Vuelta.

Europe's cycling elite went home that fall with new homework. Every director sportif, every rider, every analyst now had a name they needed to prepare for. Tadej Pogačar was no longer the kid from Slovenia with potential. He was the youngest giant the sport had seen in a long time. And what he did in Spain wasn't a one-off miracle. It was the opening chapter of something far greater.

Chapter 3
Tour de France 2020 – The Upset That Shook the World

The time-trial on La Planche des Belles Filles that rewrote Slovenian history and humbled the favorite

Nobody saw it coming, not like this. Not with the clarity of a man racing not just against time, but rewriting it. On September 19, 2020, the world watched as a 21-year-old Tadej Pogačar rode into cycling immortality on the brutal slopes of La Planche des Belles Filles. The race wasn't just about seconds or minutes anymore. It became a spectacle that rearranged the hierarchy of sport, country, and expectations.

It had been Primož Roglič's Tour to lose. For twenty days, he had led with the patience of a surgeon. His Jumbo-Visma team dominated the race, yellow-clad and meticulous, crushing climbs with clockwork precision and flattening any chaos that dared to rise. Roglič himself had been steady, never flamboyant, never flashy, but always in control. He had every reason to feel confident heading into Stage 20's individual time trial. After all, he held a 57-second lead over Pogačar. He only had to defend it over 36.2 kilometers. The final climb, La Planche des Belles Filles, was cruel, but manageable. Everyone said so. The race was his to protect. All he had to do was not crack.

That morning, Slovenia was already celebrating a moment that would enter its sporting history. Two countrymen poised to finish first and second in the world's most prestigious cycling race, a nation of barely two million producing two world-class Grand Tour riders in the same generation. For a country with no deep-rooted cycling tradition, it was unfathomable. They were already heroes. But only one would wear yellow on the Champs-Élysées.

As the race against the clock began, all eyes turned to Pogačar. He rolled out in the white skinsuit of the best young rider classification, a subtle symbol of the prodigy he was. But there was nothing youthful in the way he attacked the course. The opening section was flat, designed for specialists, yet Pogačar flew through it. No missteps, no hesitations, just relentless pedal strokes that betrayed no nerves. The first time check showed he was already gaining. The margin started to shrink.

At the roadside, the crowds were sparse, 2020 was still deep in the grip of the COVID-19 pandemic, but the tension was universal. Across Europe, across social media feeds and television broadcasts, cycling fans felt something shift. This wasn't just a good start. It was something seismic.

Halfway through the course, the numbers became impossible to ignore. Pogačar wasn't just gaining ground; he was dismantling the gap. The time trial had turned into a one-man assault on expectation. Every pedal stroke looked calculated yet untethered from fear. His cadence never dipped. His body never flailed. There was no visible strain, just laser-focused control.

Roglič, starting last, was behind him on the road and on the clock. Clad in a yellow skinsuit, he had the burden of history on his shoulders. For two years, he had climbed the rankings of world cycling, building his identity as a meticulous, unshakable force. But on that day, something looked off. His helmet tilted slightly. His face betrayed a quiet panic. The aerodynamic position he'd perfected seemed tighter, less natural. When he hit the climb, the cracks deepened.

Pogačar had already switched bikes by then. A calculated move, his time trial bike traded for a lighter road bike just before the gradient turned savage. The transition was seamless. With no hesitation, he mounted the new frame and danced up the steepest parts of the mountain. It was no longer just about time. It was poetry in motion.

On television, commentators couldn't believe what they were watching. The graphics showing time splits painted a picture that didn't match the prevailing narrative. Pogačar was not just taking back seconds. He was turning the Tour on its head.

When he crossed the line, the clock froze at 55 minutes and 55 seconds, nearly two minutes faster than the next-best time. It was a statement so loud that silence followed. For a moment, everyone paused, waiting for a correction, a recalibration. Surely, it had to be wrong.

But it wasn't.

Pogačar took off his helmet, his hair soaked in sweat, his breathing controlled. No grand celebration. No raised arms. Just a glance at the screen and a smile that looked as if he had only surprised himself.

Then came Roglič. Slower at every time check. His signature tempo cracked by the gradient and the gravity of the moment. He ground up the final meters of La Planche with a face that spoke of disbelief. The yellow jersey he had worn for eleven days was slipping away before he reached the summit. When he finally crossed the line, he stopped, not in celebration, but in silent devastation.

He had lost nearly two minutes. Pogačar, now clad in white, had taken yellow.

Cycling hadn't seen anything like it. A time trial on the penultimate day of the Tour de France, a format designed to maintain the status quo, had become a battleground for one of the greatest upsets in modern sports. It wasn't just about the youth toppling experience, or a new star being born. It was about witnessing a rider reach into his core and find something transcendent. Pogačar didn't just ride faster. He rewrote what was possible for a Grand Tour debutant.

At twenty-one, he became the youngest winner of the Tour de France since 1904. He also claimed the polka dot jersey for best climber and the white jersey for best young rider, completing a treble that hadn't been seen since Eddy Merckx in 1972. But this wasn't a product of chance or chaos. It was execution, cold, ruthless, brilliant execution, on the day it mattered most.

For Slovenia, the day was complicated. Pride in one of their own pulling off the greatest Tour de France turnaround in decades mixed with heartbreak for Roglič, a national icon who had led with dignity, grace, and incredible strength. The country didn't pick sides. They embraced both riders, knowing that this wasn't a rivalry born of animosity but a paradox of excellence.

But for the world, the stage belonged to Pogačar. The boy who had stunned the Vuelta in 2019 had now conquered the biggest race of all. And he did it not by surviving but by attacking, by riding a time trial for the ages, up a climb that had never witnessed anything quite like it.

La Planche des Belles Filles had become a stage for legend. Not because of drama or collapse, but because of clarity. It was there, on those 6 kilometers of torture and triumph, that Tadej Pogačar announced himself not just as a talent but as a force, one that would reshape cycling's future before it had even settled into the present.

How the youngest post-war champion took the biggest crown cycling has to offer

When Tadej Pogačar stepped onto the final podium in Paris, wearing the maillot jaune as the 2020 Tour de France champion, the world of cycling stood still. Not from the pageantry of the moment or the historic sweep of three classifications, but because the sport had just been cracked open by a 21-year-old who wasn't supposed to win, not yet. The youngest post-war champion hadn't merely triumphed; he had altered the gravitational center of the sport.

From the moment he claimed yellow on Stage 20 at La Planche des Belles Filles, the narrative around him could no longer be written with caution or curiosity. He was no longer a prodigy waiting his turn. He had taken the crown with the confidence of a rider twice his age. Paris was supposed to be a coronation for Primož Roglič. But as the Arc de Triomphe towered behind the final procession, it was Pogačar who carried the sun on his back, the yellow jersey that symbolizes conquest, consistency, and a rare breed of excellence.

The Tour de France is unforgiving to the inexperienced. Historically, it chews up debutants, humbles favorites, and demands years of tactical schooling. Riders typically graduate through the sport with patience: first survive, then contend, maybe someday win. Pogačar shattered that sequence like a mirror. This was his first Tour. No stage recon of the Champs-Élysées, no prior understanding of three weeks of cumulative exhaustion, no real reference point for what it means to hold your nerve over twenty-one stages of warfare. And yet, there he stood, arms aloft, smile somewhere between disbelief and composure, his white youth jersey hidden beneath cycling's most coveted garment.

He had entered the 2020 Tour as a wildcard, not a marked man. UAE Team Emirates had leadership options, but nobody expected Pogačar to be fighting for yellow. They were a young team, still building their structure around Grand Tour ambitions. His goal, as he had plainly stated at the start, was to learn. Maybe a stage win. Maybe a top ten. Nothing more.

What unfolded was a tactical masterclass wrapped in youthful audacity. He didn't lead the general classification until the penultimate day, but he never dropped far behind. Every climb became an opportunity, not a threat. On the Grand Colombier, while others conserved, he tested. On the Col de la Loze, where the gradients soared into double digits, he never surrendered more than Roglič would allow. And when given a sliver of daylight, he pounced, especially in the Pyrenees, where he clawed back time like a veteran shark circling a tired boat.

But it wasn't just how he rode; it was how he refused to ride like a newcomer. There were no nerves in his descending. No panic in his pacing. His tactics were fluid, shaped in the moment but executed with clarity. He seemed to defy the very idea that riders must "serve an apprenticeship" in Grand Tours. If he was intimidated, no one saw it. Not the cameras, not the rivals, not even his own teammates.

When the final stage rolled into Paris, the peloton softened its posture. As tradition dictates, the final day is a victory parade until the Champs-Élysées circuits. And in that golden twilight, Pogačar was surrounded by men who had tried and failed for years to reach the same peak. Riders with scars, with silver medals, with broken dreams scattered across Mont Ventoux and Alpe d'Huez. And there he was, barely older than the under-23 category, yet carrying the burden of history with the grace of a born champion.

The youngest winner of the Tour de France since Henri Cornet in 1904. The first Slovenian to claim cycling's highest honor. The only rider since Eddy Merckx to win the yellow, polka dot, and white jerseys in the same edition. These were more than stats. They were seismic cracks in what had seemed to be the natural order. For decades, Tour champions were forged over years, months of altitude camps, a meticulous team, seasoned sports directors, calculated marginal gains. Pogačar tore through that narrative with raw talent, decisive aggression, and a spirit that never wavered.

Many tried to explain it. Some credited his calm demeanor. Others pointed to his unconventional training during lockdown. A few, behind closed doors, whispered whether what they had witnessed could be real. The numbers told no lies. His power output on climbs matched the elite. His time trial efficiency was surgical. There were no red flags. Just a rider operating at a frequency nobody else could touch.

What makes his youth so startling is how complete his skillset already appeared. Most riders need years to learn how to ride in crosswinds, to descend at 90 kilometers per hour without fear, to suffer through week three with an iron stomach. Pogačar had it all. He attacked like a climber, time trialed like a diesel engine, and managed his efforts like a rider who had read every Tour script ever written. Only he never followed the script. He authored a new one.

Slovenia erupted with pride. Flags lined the streets in Komenda and Klanec. Murals began appearing on walls that had never known graffiti. Children asked for bikes instead of video games. For a small country nestled between Italy, Austria, and Hungary, its new champion had become more than a sports star, he had become a symbol. Not just of possibility, but of self-belief.

His family watched from home. COVID restrictions barred them from Paris. His parents, Mirjam and Marjan, cried in their living room, watching their son break barriers not even they could have imagined. His brother Tilen sat speechless, thinking about the boy who once rode behind him, trying to keep up, trying to mimic his cadence. The boy had become a king.

Journalists scrambled to interview him, and Pogačar, ever humble, didn't gloat. His post-race words carried the same honesty that had marked his riding. "I think I'm dreaming," he said. But he wasn't. He had taken yellow, not stolen it. He hadn't waited for Roglič to falter, he had seized his moment with clarity and courage.

As the Slovenian national anthem played over the Place de la Concorde, and Pogačar stood at the top step of the podium, something shifted in professional cycling. Not just because the race had a new winner, but because the next generation had announced its arrival with thunder. The age of methodical dominance had been disrupted by something purer, an audacious kind of brilliance that needed no preamble.

Tadej Pogačar didn't just win the Tour de France at 21. He gave it back the sense of magic that only youth, bravery, and breathtaking talent can bring. He wore yellow, not just because he finished first, but because he lit up the sport with the glow of a new era.

The humility, humor, and disbelief that made fans fall in love with Pogačar overnight

Tadej Pogačar's astonishing victory in the 2020 Tour de France rewrote the script for what a Grand Tour champion could be. Not only because of his youth or the sheer drama of his Stage 20 takeover, but because of the person behind the performance. Once the yellow jersey settled on his shoulders and the global media spotlight came into full focus, the world discovered that Pogačar wasn't just a gifted rider, he was disarmingly human. He didn't act like someone who had just made history. He joked, he smiled sheepishly, he downplayed his achievements with a kind of modesty that felt rare in professional sport. What followed wasn't just admiration for what he had done; it was affection for who he was.

On the Paris podium, with champagne in hand and cameras clicking endlessly, he looked more like a kid invited to a grown-up party than the youngest winner of cycling's greatest race in over a century. He didn't perform or dramatize. When asked what he was feeling, he shrugged with a small laugh and said, "I don't know what to say. I think I need some time to understand this." The words weren't rehearsed. They were raw. He wasn't trying to be humble. He simply was.

What caught people off guard was the contrast between the warrior they had watched over 21 grueling stages and the wide-eyed, boyish figure smiling at the top step of the podium. The image of him holding the yellow, polka dot, and white jerseys should have screamed dominance. Instead, it felt like a Cinderella moment, except the slippers were cleated, and the carriage was a Cervélo.

Journalists, expecting tightly wound statements or team-scripted platitudes, were met with refreshingly honest answers. One reporter asked if he had dreamt of this moment his whole life. Pogačar smiled and replied, "Not really. I only started cycling because my brother did. I didn't expect to be here this fast." There was no attempt to craft mythology. He seemed as surprised as everyone else that he had just become the new face of a global sport.

During interviews, he often giggled at questions or deflected compliments with unexpected self-deprecation. When praised for his legendary time trial, he looked genuinely embarrassed, scratching the back of his neck and replying, "I just rode as hard as I could. I didn't think it would be enough." This wasn't a carefully orchestrated PR act. It was simply Tadej, unfiltered and genuine.

The disbelief he carried wasn't false humility; it was the reflection of a young man whose rise had been so meteoric that even he hadn't caught up to it emotionally. This authenticity became magnetic. Fans who had never followed cycling were suddenly Googling his name. Veteran followers of the sport, accustomed to calculated personas, found themselves charmed. Social media lit up not only with praise for his riding, but with memes and gifs of his facial expressions, his bashful smiles, and his press conference bloopers.

One particular moment that encapsulated his appeal came on the morning after the final stage, during a post-race media interview. Asked how he had celebrated, he admitted he had eaten "some chips and pizza," before pausing and adding with a grin, "Maybe too much." It was the kind of answer that made fans laugh, not because it was strategic, but because it was so ordinary. He had just conquered the Tour de France, and his idea of indulgence was a junk-food binge and a good night's sleep.

His teammates spoke of the same warmth behind the scenes. They described him as someone who never carried himself like a star, even after Paris. He helped clean his own bottles. He thanked mechanics and soigneurs personally after every stage. He joked around during warm-ups and treated every member of the UAE Team Emirates staff with unchanging respect, regardless of his growing stature. Riders often change once they win. Pogačar, they said, didn't.

What also won hearts was his openness about emotion. He didn't mask tears. He wasn't afraid to say he was nervous, or that he missed home. When asked about riding without fans during the pandemic-limited edition of the Tour, he spoke not just about the empty roads but about missing the energy, the smiles, the little kids waving flags. He talked like someone who loved the sport not for the fame, but for the connection. That attitude resonated, especially in 2020, a year of isolation, distance, and grief.

In a sport often shadowed by cynicism, especially when a new champion emerges unexpectedly, Pogačar's transparent joy helped cut through the skepticism. When rivals were asked about him, they rarely offered guarded responses. They smiled. Richie Porte, who also stood on the Paris podium that year, called him "a breath of fresh air." Others echoed that sentiment. He wasn't arrogant. He wasn't rehearsed. He was a kid doing what he loved, and doing it better than anyone.

His humor became a subtle but defining feature. During a post-Tour interview when asked what he would do with the prize money, he quipped, "Maybe buy a PlayStation." He laughed again when someone asked if he now considered himself the best rider in the world. "Oh no," he said. "There are too many strong guys. I just had one good race." It wasn't false modesty. He genuinely didn't place himself above others. That humility, paired with his dry, understated jokes, made him feel like a friend more than a figurehead.

Outside of the sport, people from all over began reaching out. Parents whose kids had started riding bikes again. Teenagers who saw in him a different kind of hero, quiet, awkward, but determined and kind. His win didn't just inspire future cyclists; it inspired a different vision of what greatness could look like.

He never tried to dominate the room. He didn't raise his voice. His power came not from chest-thumping but from silent conviction. And when he spoke, you listened, not because he demanded attention, but because his authenticity invited it. That quality didn't fade after Paris. It traveled with him to every race that followed, and it began with that stunning, surreal summer in France.

As the Eiffel Tower glowed behind him and the Tour de France trophy gleamed in the fading light, Tadej Pogačar smiled for the cameras. But it was the same smile he'd shown in the Slovenian hills, the same one from the day he first joined Rog, the same one he wore crossing the line in Stage 20. Nothing had changed him, not the podium, not the headlines, not the mountain he had just climbed. That constancy was what made people believe in him, not just as a champion, but as a human being they could trust, cheer for, and celebrate without reservation. It wasn't the yellow jersey that made Tadej Pogačar loved. It was the humility beneath it.

Chapter 4
Repeating the Impossible

How Tadej crushed doubts and defended his title with calculated brilliance

After stunning the world in 2020, Tadej Pogačar faced a different kind of mountain in 2021: expectation. The young Slovenian who had shocked the cycling world with a time trial for the ages now wore the weight of the yellow jersey before the first pedal stroke of the Tour de France that summer. What he had done at La Planche des Belles Filles had felt like lightning. But lightning, people whispered, rarely strikes twice. Could he do it again? Could he withstand a field now fully aware of what he was capable of?

Tadej arrived at the Grand Départ in Brest not as the underdog, but as the hunted. He was no longer the cheerful surprise; he was the reigning champion, the man with a target on his back. The race would feature rivals old and new, Primož Roglič still simmering from the heartbreak of the previous year, Geraint Thomas looking to reclaim former glories, and a resurgent Richard Carapaz with Ineos Grenadiers plotting every move with clinical precision. Pogačar knew this time would be different. There would be no hiding, no room for mistakes, and absolutely no excuse.

Yet from the very first stages, he exuded calm. No frantic effort to dominate early. No showboating. He let the chaos play out around him. The opening week was marred by crashes and unpredictability, taking out several major names, including Roglič, who suffered injuries that would slowly end his bid for revenge. Tadej avoided most of the chaos, guided by a UAE Team Emirates squad that many analysts had labeled as too thin, too unproven to support a yellow jersey defense. But Pogačar didn't need babysitting, he needed only moments. And when the race reached the time trial on Stage 5, he delivered the first of many.

That day, between Changé and Laval, Pogačar didn't just ride well, he dismantled the clock. His performance in the 27.2 km time trial was near-flawless, with aerodynamic mastery, pedal cadence, and positional awareness that made observers shake their heads. Riders expected to gain time on him lost it. Those hoping to cling on fell further behind. By the end of that stage, he had sent a warning: 2020 wasn't a fluke, and this time, he was stronger.

The deeper the race went, the clearer it became that he wasn't reacting, he was dictating. The Alps came, and with them, the real tests. On Stage 8 to Le Grand-Bornand, under cold rain and over brutal climbs, Tadej launched what would become the defining attack of the Tour. With over 30 kilometers still to race, he attacked on the Col de Romme, not because he needed to, but because he could. It was a bold, risky move that reminded everyone watching that Pogačar wasn't just talented, he was fearless. That day, he didn't simply take the yellow jersey; he seized control of the race. And from that point on, he never let go.

His climbing was almost theatrical in its ease. He danced on the pedals on the Col du Portet, rode with serenity up Luz Ardiden, and looked over his shoulder not in worry, but in disbelief that no one could follow. Carapaz tried to bluff him. Vingegaard surged in the Pyrenees. But whenever danger approached, Pogačar answered with economy and force. He rode with the intelligence of a veteran and the legs of a phenom.

There was no miracle stage this time. No come-from-behind drama. This was domination by design. At just 22 years old, he was riding with composure that belied his youth. It wasn't a show. It was a masterclass. Each move was measured. Every attack was timed. He wasn't simply racing rivals; he was outmaneuvering an entire peloton shaped to beat him.

Doubters, once vocal, began to fade. The idea that his 2020 win had been circumstantial collapsed under the weight of his consistency. He wasn't just defending the yellow jersey, he was redefining what defending meant. Never rattled. Never reckless. Always ready.

Stage 17 to the Col du Portet, deep in the Pyrenees, put his grit on full display. Carapaz and Vingegaard tried to isolate him, launching coordinated attacks in the final kilometers. They pushed, teased, and tested him. Tadej didn't panic. He sat calmly on their wheels. Then, with 800 meters to go, he surged, not out of desperation, but like a chess player tipping the board. The move was cold, calculated, and completely demoralizing. The moment he crossed the line, pumping his fist, it was clear: this wasn't a kid catching lightning. This was a champion building a dynasty.

But for all his ferocity on the mountains, it was his demeanor off the bike that continued to win hearts. His interviews were light, often humorous, never inflated. When asked if he felt pressure carrying the yellow jersey for so many days, he smiled and said, "Not really, I just try to enjoy it. It's a beautiful jersey." There was no trace of arrogance, no rehearsed defiance to critics. He let his legs do the talking and his personality do the connecting.

By the time he rolled into Paris in yellow again, holding both the polka dot and white jerseys, it was clear the sport was witnessing a generational force. He didn't just win the Tour, he erased doubt, silenced cynics, and proved that brilliance doesn't need an origin story filled with hardship or mythology. Sometimes, it comes from joy, clarity, and relentless work.

Tadej didn't raise his arms in flamboyant celebration during the final stage. He soaked in the moment, exchanging smiles with teammates, joking with riders he had just defeated, and looking more like a college student on a summer adventure than a two-time Tour champion. That contradiction, his quiet nature paired with crushing talent, had become his signature.

The 2021 Tour de France didn't just mark the continuation of a dream; it confirmed the beginning of a new era. He wasn't the one-hit wonder. He was the real thing. And as he stood atop the podium, once again bathed in yellow beneath the Parisian sun, the cycling world knew that the era of doubt was over. This was not luck. This was the birth of a legend who wasn't done climbing.

How his daring solo wins on stages like Col du Portet left rivals gasping and spectators roaring

By the time Tadej Pogačar crested the summit of Col du Portet during the 2021 Tour de France, the mystique surrounding him had evolved into something almost mythological. It wasn't just that he won; it was how he did it, like a rider born in thinner air, molded by slopes and gradients that caused others to unravel. That day on the mountain, he didn't merely take time; he seized belief, crushed resistance, and made one of the Tour's most brutal ascents look like a rite of passage he had already conquered in his dreams.

Mountains were never just terrain for Pogačar. They were invitations. While some riders feared them and others merely endured, he danced with them. His relationship with elevation wasn't about surviving climbs, it was about using them to reveal who he truly was. From the early days in Slovenia, where he would pedal up the jagged hills outside Klanec just to chase his brother, something in him had been drawn to ascent. On grand stages, that instinct became weaponized.

Stage 17 of the 2021 Tour de France was not a place where reputations were gently tested, it was where careers could crumble. The route from Muret to Saint-Lary-Soulan, finishing atop the Col du Portet, was carved in cruelty. Over 170 kilometers of attritional road, the final 16 kilometers alone packed with punishing ramps that flirted with double-digit gradients. The Pyrenees are infamous for delivering drama; on this day, they delivered a coronation.

Pogačar didn't need to win that stage. He already held the yellow jersey. His lead was sufficient. Caution would have been rational. But he chose poetry instead of prudence. The early part of the climb saw him shadowed by Jonas Vingegaard and Richard Carapaz. The trio dropped everyone else, forming a high-altitude chessboard in motion. Carapaz played games, riding erratically, testing, feinting. Vingegaard remained calm but visibly strained. And Pogačar, he just kept breathing through his nose, looking over his shoulder, not with fear, but almost curiosity, as though wondering when they would break.

With a little over 800 meters remaining, he stopped wondering.

He rose from the saddle, exploded forward, and opened a gap that never shrank. There was no hesitation, no glance backward, no mercy. The television cameras could barely keep up. The fans lining the barriers went from screaming to stunned. Commentators ran out of superlatives. This was no attack, it was an announcement: the mountains were his, and anyone who tried to trespass would have to pay a toll in oxygen and resolve.

His face, captured as he crossed the line, said it all. No wild celebration, just a clenched fist and a look of raw defiance. It was personal. Not because someone had doubted him, but because the mountain had dared to ask a question, and he had responded with a roar.

Pogačar's relationship with these high-altitude battlegrounds went beyond physical preparation. His climbing wasn't just strength, it was rhythm, timing, intuition. Where others planned wattage zones and power outputs, he read the road like an artist reads a canvas. And his strokes were bold, attacks that seemed too early, surges that looked unsustainable, yet he made them stick, not with brute force, but with a serenity that unsettled his rivals.

After the Col du Portet masterclass, people began comparing him not just to champions but to legends. Names like Pantani and Merckx started to resurface. Not because he mimicked them, but because he was building his own style, modern, data-aware, yet fearless in a way the sport had not seen for decades. He was a climber in the old sense: willing to take risks, unafraid to lose, and utterly at home when the road turned skyward.

The legacy of that ride stretched far beyond that one summit. It changed how teams planned their future rosters. It altered tactics across the peloton. It reminded fans that cycling, at its best, is not only a battle of endurance but of spirit. Tadej didn't need altitude to showcase dominance, but under the rarefied air of the Pyrenees, his brilliance became impossible to ignore.

He followed up the Col du Portet spectacle with another solo effort at Luz Ardiden. Again, he didn't have to attack. Again, he did. Because he could. The yellow jersey on his back didn't weigh him down, it propelled him forward. He rode as though gravity affected him differently, as though the higher he went, the lighter his burdens became. That psychological edge, his refusal to play defensive, shattered traditional expectations. He wasn't protecting a title; he was reinventing how it could be claimed.

What made it all the more staggering was his age. Riders are not supposed to dominate climbs like this at 22. They are not supposed to look this untroubled, this precise, this fearless. Yet there he was, cresting summit after summit like he had written the gradients himself. He turned brutal profiles into playgrounds and invited everyone to watch his joy unfold.

His UAE Team Emirates squad did what they could to support him. But on those steep inclines, when the domestiques peeled away, it was just him and the mountain. And every time, he chose confrontation. Not out of ego, but because the road dared him to. And with each dare, he responded, not with words, but with pedals.

Spectators began to arrive earlier each day just to catch a glimpse of him on the switchbacks. Children waved signs with his name, old fans clutched Slovenian flags, and roadside chants echoed his nickname, "Pogi!", like a hymn. The mountains weren't just where he won; they were where he bonded with the world.

When the 2021 Tour de France concluded, it wasn't just his victory that made headlines. It was the manner in which he had dismantled the race, brick by brick, climb by climb. His ascents weren't mechanical, they were emotional journeys. Each one told a story of courage, timing, and belief.

The mountain stages, once feared by even the strongest contenders, had become a stage for his soul. And the Col du Portet stood above them all, not because it gave him the most time, but because it revealed the most truth. That day, a boy from Klanec who once pedaled uphill chasing his brother showed the world that the sky wasn't his limit, it was his home.

Dominating both yellow and polka dot classifications: a rare mastery few had ever seen

The sight of Tadej Pogačar on the Champs-Élysées in 2021 wasn't just memorable for the glint of the yellow jersey under the Parisian sun. What turned heads, what made jaws drop even among hardened veterans of the sport, was the polka-dotted jersey he held over his arm, the one reserved for the King of the Mountains. It wasn't supposed to happen this way. Not because he wasn't capable, but because modern cycling, with all its tactical specializations and dedicated domestiques, made this kind of double almost unthinkable. Yet there he was, smiling modestly, holding the symbols of dominance over two of the sport's most revered battlegrounds: the overall Tour de France and the high mountains that once humbled legends.

Only a handful of riders in cycling history had ever pulled off such a feat. Eddy Merckx did it. So did Fausto Coppi and Gino Bartali, names that exist in the pantheon of myth. For a 22-year-old Slovenian to add his name to that list required not just talent, but something closer to defiance, against logic, against fatigue, against history itself.

He didn't chase both jerseys from the outset. That wasn't the plan. Riders rarely admit targeting the polka dots when their sights are set on yellow. The two goals demand opposing rhythms. Yellow is earned through consistency, control, and strategic bursts across three weeks of chaos. The polka dot jersey, meanwhile, is usually claimed through relentless attacks on categorized climbs, a style that burns energy rather than conserves it. The very idea that someone could master both on the same journey felt like trying to sprint while simultaneously pacing a marathon. Yet Pogačar redefined what control and aggression could look like when carried in the same frame.

The 2021 Tour de France laid out a brutal canvas. There were summit finishes across the Alps and the Pyrenees, high-altitude tests that punished anyone who misjudged effort by even a few seconds. Riders aimed their calendars at select stages, carefully choosing when to unleash. Pogačar didn't wait for permission. On the Col de Romme and the Col de la Colombière during Stage 8, while rivals were still gauging each other, he attacked with venom. That move not only reshaped the general classification, it scored massive King of the Mountains points. He wasn't just distancing himself from challengers in the GC; he was quietly stacking up points where few expected him to.

His rides up the Col du Portet and Luz Ardiden were even more definitive. These weren't just mountain-top victories; they were moments of absolute control. Every hairpin bend he conquered alone meant not just minutes gained in the GC but precious mountain points that elevated him into polka dot territory. Unlike pure climbers who throw everything into those stages hoping to survive the time trials, Pogačar seemed to glide through them like he was built differently. He didn't accumulate the jersey points by grinding for them day after day, he won them by being untouchable when it mattered most.

There was something beautifully paradoxical about his dominance. He rode with a grace that made brutal climbs seem less like torture and more like movement poetry. Yet the scoreboard told a harsher truth: he was dismantling his opponents. They weren't losing because they were weak. They were losing because they were riding in the same race as someone who had made evolution look like a personal project.

Wearing yellow and holding polka dot didn't just represent strength, it symbolized strategic brilliance. He didn't need to wear the King of the Mountains jersey to climb like one. But once it became mathematically possible, once his points were uncatchable, it felt like a quiet nod to the purists, the ones who still believed that greatness meant conquering everything, not just what was necessary.

There was a deeper symbolism too. The polka dots are often romanticized. They're not just about power; they're about pain and perseverance, about those who find transcendence in altitude. To win them while also being the most consistent, most complete rider in the race? That was poetry delivered by legs and lungs. It was almost sacrilegious, like stealing fire from the gods and then riding away with it smiling.

For younger fans, many of whom had never seen such dual mastery live, this was more than a performance, it was a re-education. The idea that a modern rider could touch every domain, from time trials to mountaintops, and still remain humble, even joyful, reshaped their expectations. And for older fans, especially those who'd lived through eras of heartbreak and suspicion, it was a moment of restored belief. Watching Pogačar ride solo over summit finishes, with nothing but wind and willpower surrounding him, felt like seeing the sport dream again.

The team around him, UAE Team Emirates, played a supportive role, but even they admitted they weren't quite expecting this scope of brilliance. They had backed him to defend his yellow jersey. They didn't foresee he'd also lay claim to the hills, the heartbreak, and the heroism of the race's most brutal ascents. His double haul wasn't built on careful defense, it was carved out of boldness.

What made it even more remarkable was how effortlessly he carried it. He didn't boast. He didn't point fingers. He joked with reporters. He took selfies with fans. When asked about the history he'd joined, he smiled as if he was being complimented for remembering to return a shopping cart. The weight of double jerseys didn't seem to bend his back. They hung on him like armor and wings at once.

As the race wrapped and the jerseys were officially awarded, there was a surreal moment when Pogačar stood on the podium wearing yellow, holding polka dots, and smiling with the white jersey for best young rider waiting for him backstage. Three jerseys. One rider. It was dominance disguised as joy, control wrapped in charm. No one could touch him, not on paper, not on pavement, not even in spirit.

People often talk about legends as though they belong to the past. That summer, as Pogačar rode away from the peloton and into pages of cycling's most sacred scripts, he reminded everyone that sometimes, the great ones don't just return, they arrive young, ride with wonder, and rewrite what was thought to be impossible.

Chapter 5
The Rivalry That Redefined the Tour

The thrilling new duel that revived Tour de France drama for a new generation

For years, the Tour de France seemed to flirt with predictability. Dominance had become a double-edged sword, admired, but sterile. Superteams crushed resistance, and the yellow jersey often felt like it was settled before the Alps. Then came Tadej Pogačar, a hurricane of unpredictability in a sport obsessed with control. But what no one expected was that his brightest spark would ignite even more furiously when met with quiet, surgical resistance. That resistance wore the name Jonas Vingegaard, and together they brought back the fire the Tour had been missing.

It wasn't a rivalry born of animosity. There was no venom in their eyes, no media-fueled war of words. What set them apart was respect, and what made them unforgettable was how they exposed each other's limits and then crossed their own. The world hadn't seen a head-to-head like this in cycling's grandest race for decades, not since the Hinault vs. Fignon days, not since Contador vs. Schleck briefly lit up the Pyrenees. Vingegaard and Pogačar created something purer, more elemental: the feeling that anything could happen at any moment.

The duel first took on real shape during the 2022 Tour. By then, Pogačar was the reigning monarch, two-time champion, seemingly bulletproof. He won early. He smiled often. He looked like a man stretching his legs rather than defending a crown. But behind him rode a lean, inconspicuous Dane with glacier-cool focus and a devastating ability to bide time. Vingegaard wasn't loud. He didn't attack for show. He simply watched. Waited. Calculated. Until Stage 11, when the balance shifted.

That day on the Col du Granon rewrote expectations. While Pogačar pushed to control the race, launching attacks and chasing threats, Vingegaard rode with sniper-like patience. When the moment came, he struck, not recklessly, but with precision. Pogačar cracked. It was the first time the cycling world had seen him falter so visibly. Sweat ran faster than his cadence. His jersey sagged, not in fabric but in fear. And when Vingegaard crossed the line solo, the torch hadn't just been touched, it had been contested.

The 2022 Tour belonged to Vingegaard, but it didn't feel like a dethroning. It felt like a beginning. The Dane had taken yellow, but Pogačar had lost nothing of his luster. What unfolded over the remainder of the race was less about defeat and more about defiance. The Slovenian attacked again and again, not to win, but to let the world know he wasn't done. Their duel wasn't a question of who had more titles, it was about who had more heart.

By 2023, fans no longer watched the Tour for spectacle. They watched it for this rivalry. Vingegaard vs. Pogačar had become cycling's new heartbeat, its north star. Even casual viewers could name them both. Kids in playgrounds mimicked their sprints. Journalists wrote previews not about team strategies, but about moments where their wheels might align again. It was tennis' Federer vs. Nadal, but on tarmac and at altitude.

Stage after stage, they danced with danger. On mountain summits and windy flats, in blistering heat and through tunnelled crowds, they traded punches without trading pride. There was no need for mind games. Their rivalry was inked in kilometers, not controversy.

Vingegaard was the surgeon, measured, economical, unshakable. Pogačar was the artist, restless, inspired, prone to bursts that made no tactical sense but left fans breathless. One rode with the pulse of the peloton. The other rode with the pulse of his soul.

The 2023 duel hit its crescendo in the high Alps. Pogačar had landed early blows, reclaiming seconds here and there. Then came Stage 17, and the Tourmalet, and the long, grinding climb to Courchevel. Vingegaard unleashed one of the most devastating time trial performances in modern history, his cadence like clockwork, his breathing never labored. Pogačar, normally a master of the hurt zone, looked suddenly mortal. Grit faded into pain. The gap widened. The yellow jersey tilted again toward Denmark.

But even then, fans didn't turn away. If anything, they leaned in closer. Because what defined this rivalry wasn't just the moments one crushed the other, it was what followed. The day after Pogačar cracked, he bounced back with a smile, telling reporters, "I'm gone. I'm dead." He laughed at himself, not because he didn't care, but because he knew the beauty of vulnerability. It's what made him beloved, and what made Vingegaard's stoic brilliance shine even brighter beside it.

They pushed each other into greatness. Each knew he wouldn't have reached such rarefied air without the other's shadow looming. There was no complacency. There was no dominance without resistance. Vingegaard didn't just beat Pogačar. He elevated him. And Pogačar, with every insane counterattack, every grin through the sweat, made Vingegaard's calm menace even more riveting.

The rivalry spilled beyond the Tour. Monuments, classics, even smaller stage races became proxy battles. Fans parsed training photos for hints. Social media became a scoreboard. But unlike rivalries steeped in ego, theirs never lost humanity. When

Vingegaard waited for Pogačar after a crash, it wasn't for headlines, it was for honor. When they shook hands at the podium, it wasn't for protocol, it was a gesture of survival, of respect earned the hard way.

Their duel revived something ancient in cycling: the idea that winning matters, but the fight matters more. It reminded people that greatness isn't just about what you accomplish alone, it's what you draw out of your rival. For a sport scarred by suspicion and often divided by tactics, they offered clarity. You didn't need to be Slovenian or Danish to feel invested. You just had to love the purity of sport.

As of now, the ledger still shifts. One year Vingegaard, the next maybe Pogačar. But no one wants it to end. Because every time they line up at the start, the world watches not to see who wins, but to witness the moments that might make history blush. The rivalry isn't just redefining the Tour. It's reminding us why we watch. Why we believe. Why, deep down, we all still hope for a duel on a mountaintop that makes us feel alive.

How losing the Tour sharpened his hunger and transformed his strategy

The day Pogačar stood on the final podium in Paris in 2022, silver medals in hand and a quiet look etched across his face, it wasn't defeat that defined him, it was the hunger that followed. He had come so close, only to be outmaneuvered by Jonas Vingegaard and relegated to second place. The result stung, etched deep by the world watching. Yet the profound pain became the kindling that would refill his internal fire, reshaping his mindset and painting a precise map for his return.

The ride itself had been brutal. Pogačar had started aggressively, launching attacks on multiple stages, forcing Vingegaard into defense. He had tested the waters, probing for weaknesses, hoping for cracks. But for every punch he threw, Vingegaard absorbed and countered with ice-cold revenge. Stage after stage, the Slovenian's efforts were met with measured resistance. Watching his rival ride through pain without losing power or composure shifted something in Pogačar's approach. He realized that bravery alone wouldn't be enough; he would need patience, calculation, and the tactical savvy to win when it mattered most.

Paris wasn't his moment in 2022, but the hours and days that followed became even more important. He retreated, silently, into reflection. Back in Slovenia, training rides that were usually serene turned into sessions of quiet intensity. Cols he had once toyed with became cages he forced himself out of, not with speed but with repeated pressure. He concentrated on pacing, on mental resilience, on reconditioning his body to resist fatigue deep into each stage. Solo rides became meditative reconstructions of every error he had made, emotional echoes of moments when he pushed too early or too late.

One of the biggest lessons he learned was resource management. He had always ridden with power and passion, but he realized that the margin between acceleration and collapse could be thinner than the break of dawn. Vingegaard's command of timing made the difference. So Pogačar began working closely with team strategists and even unorthodox advisors, sports psychologists, altitude specialists, sleep scientists, crafting what would become one of the most sophisticated Grand Tour setups ever assembled. Every detail mattered: hydration cues, nutrient timing, power output forks, bike swap protocols, even wrist position for aerodynamics. He exorcised complacency; he idolized detail.

The 2023 season unfolded as a laboratory. Early races were not just about wins, they were stress tests. When he attacked on stages of the Dauphiné or Romand, it wasn't just to impress, it was to experiment. Could he do it earlier? Could he produce the same explosive power without compromising integrity in week three? Those months were a mental and physiological reorientation. He rode with purpose beyond podiums, with questions riding beside cadence. How does pain feel at altitude? How can oxygen uptake be maximized 24 seconds earlier? Can concentration be sustained through crosswinds when the team dissolves?

The Tour rolled out in July 2023, and the transformation was already visible. From Stage 1, Pogačar didn't race like a man defending reputation, he raced like someone who had rebuilt it. He attacked when senses told him it was strategic, not just inspired. One day, he surged to drop Vingegaard on a short, sharp climb. Another, he settled calmly in yellow, refusing to panic even when others tried to spark discord. His responses were sharper, his moves quieter but more deadly. He held back from heroic reversals, chasing control rather than drama.

The Alps came again, and everything gated together. When Vingegaard attacked on Col de la Loze, Pogačar didn't throw himself after him. Instead, he found his rhythm, matched wattage per kilo, and struck back when the Dane's pace wavered. It wasn't pure strength. It was nurtured resilience, born from months spent reconstructing failure into strategy.

That stage was the pivot, not because he took yellow, but because he took confidence. For the first time since time-trialing stage 20 in 2020, Pogačar felt unafraid in the mountains. The fear of trying and failing had changed into a hunger for precision. He'd learned how to make each pedal stroke matter. His team reported a new rider: vigilant, focused, alert to slightest tilt in wind, incline, opportunity.

Even roads he had suffered on before began to feel familiar. He visualized them at dawn, turning courses into maps of emotion and energy. As stage after stage unfolded, he rode like a man who refused to leave anything to fate. Yellow trembled beneath him, and polka dots felt like an old friendship again. Hoovered by self-belief, he reclaimed every time gap with method. He didn't outrun Vingegaard on every slope, but he drew breath where his rival gasped. He seized seconds where he once released them.

Once in Paris, as he stood atop the podium again, this time alone in yellow, the victory felt different. The medals clashed with memory, but Pogačar was no longer chasing validation. He stood there with the distance of a spent winter between heartbreak and triumph. He had returned not just as a champion but as a student of loss, who had sharpened his edges so finely that even chance had to yield.

The ache of defeat had done what comfort could not. It bolstered humility, focused insight, respect for strategy. It taught endurance could be mental as much as physical. And most importantly, it established a new dimension to his legacy: that true greatness isn't just born in victory, it's reborn from adversity. From heartbreak, he had sculpted hunger; not reckless, but refined. And in the process, he gave the world not another win, but a model of transformation, wildly human, fearfully crafted, and impossible to deny.

Behind-the-scenes respect and tension between two of cycling's fiercest and finest competitors

Respect Between Jonas Vingegaard and Tadej Pogačar transcends the typical dynamic of champions competing for glory. There's a raw electricity in the air whenever they wheel alongside one another, an unspoken acknowledgment that, beneath all the tactics and theatrics, they are two giants grazing the same rare air. Their rivalry is carved from intensity, but it's guided by a profound regard forged out of equal parts admiration and uncompromising competition.

It began as a tentative dance, first glimpsed during the Alps of the 2022 Tour de France. Jonas and Tadej size each other up not through words but through every surge, every gear change, every sprint or response to a climb. They harbor an acute awareness of what the other can do: Vingegaard knows all too well how Pogačar can attack without warning, how he recovers with ease, how he transforms desperation into opportunity. Pogačar, for his part, sees in Vingegaard a spectral shade of resolve, no flinching, no wasted movement, just serialized determination.

That mutual perception isn't theoretical. It plays out in split-second decisions on the road. When Jonas makes what looks like an impulsive acceleration, it's almost never impulsive. He's tested the wattage behind that surge countless times in his preparation, calibrated it against gradients and wind, and pressed the button precisely when he knows Pogačar will notice. Conversely, Tadej reads Vingegaard's tantrums as barometers of fatigue. He's the only rider who will look at a hard Danesque attack and sit in, deliberately letting the energy hang in the air like a challenge waiting to be accepted.

Behind the scenes, riders talk about tension, but it's not acrimonious. It's respectful. That classic sports adage, "Maybe he will break, maybe he won't, but you'd better be ready", describes their relationship better than any catchy quote. It's why cameras occasionally catch them swapping glances during warm-ups, nodding without conversation. There's understanding in that nod: I see you. I feel you. I've felt that pain.

Their interaction on the road has carved deeper respect. After Stages in the Pyrenees or the Alps, it's not uncommon to see them cross paths near team buses, offering brief smiles or fist bumps. They're competitors, yes, but they're also the only two riders in the world who have proven capable of pushing the Tour boundaries, year after year, attack after attack. When one falls, the other has been there. Too early? Not early enough? Too much? Not enough? They both inhabit those margins, and with that shared space comes a bond that's rugged, unsentimental, but real.

In the lead-up to decisive stages, team briefings are soaked in strategy. Pogačar's sports directors pore over wind patterns, gradients, nutrition protocols, all targeted at gaining any edge. Vingegaard's camp does the same, knowing they're the standard he must meet, or exceed. Yet, paradoxically, each rider's success depends on the other's excellence. A lackluster Vingegaard makes Pogačar into a villain; a passive Pogačar erases Vingegaard's narrative. Their performances are interlinked, like reflected images in two mirrors facing each other.

They've never had a public battle of words. No feuds, no personal jabs. When journalists ask tough questions, both respond with courtesy. Neither relishes casting dirt on the other, even if the stakes are 100 seconds of yellow. When Pogačar lost the Tour in 2022, his first praise was for Vingegaard's ride. Vingegaard, on hearing this in the mixed zone, simply nodded at the reporters. There was no smugness. The subtext was, "I chased a man, not a myth."

Their training camps carry echoes of competitive electricity. Teammates recount sessions where they end up riding alone with their rivals because they've ridden off the bunch together, one slow, one fast, but two men leading the pack on silent respect. Each time they emerge separated by seconds, they pause at the finish, breathe, and exchange a silent acknowledgment. Not a smile of friendship. Not a nod of truce. But the quiet glance of two warriors who have measured each other's blades, and found them equally sharp.

One of the most telling episodes came off-camera at a rest day in 2023. The riders found themselves seated near each other at dinner. Their conversation wasn't prolonged or intimate, but it was revealing. Pogačar casually mentioned something from their Stage 8 encounter, how Vingegaard's move on a short climb nearly took him by surprise. Jonas didn't shift uncomfortably. He answered directly, complimenting Tadej's reaction time and attitude during the feed zone. No pretense. No competitiveness bleeding into social space. Two men projecting no heat but infinite depth.

Every time their wheels sync on steep ascents or windy plains, they put on a masterclass. They trade places; they probe each other's limits; they force smaller riders to choose which way to gas. When one makes a move, the other's response becomes a chess piece in motion, and the board tilts on pacing, blocking, and breaking. That tactical friction, born out of respect, is pure drama. And fans feel it, even if they aren't career strategists. It makes ordinary climbs historic and every breakaway plausible.

They've made cycling courageous again. Because when two riders can claw, counterattack, and still share the same space with respect, it does more than showcase athleticism, it revives humanity inside competition. People talk about their rivalry as if it has an X-factor. They're both world-class. They both press limits. They both possess united hunger and humility. And yet, they still manage to surprise each other, and the world, every time their wheels cross.

It will never be a rivalry defined by publication or scandal. It doesn't need noise. It's grounded in flesh and bone: two men who hurt, sweat, calculate, and attack in light of each other's excellence. No doubt one day they will stand side by side on a podium again. Maybe one will beat the other. Maybe both will share the yellow. Win or lose, the handshakes, the nods, the words, those reflections of respect, will tell the story deeper than any headlines. Because when lions duel, their respect grows strongest after war, and the King? He's crowned not just by victory, but by the opponent who allowed him to fight.

Chapter 6
From Monuments to Masterpieces

How gravel roads and guts gave him one of the most unforgettable solo wins of all time

Tadej Pogačar's victory at the 2023 Strade Bianche has become one of the defining performances of his career. Gravel roads that wind through the Tuscan countryside, notorious for their irregular surfaces and steep climbs, often shape the riders who tackle them. In Poggibonsi, held on March 4, 2023, Pogačar turned the iconic Strade Bianche into his personal gallery, crafting a solo masterpiece that remains etched in cycling memory.

The Strade Bianche isn't like any other classic. Its paths are unpaved, often dusty or muddy, depending on the weather. They bend and roll, with short, sharp climbs, called "cotes", that pack more suffering than many Alpine ascents. It demands resilience and technical skill far beyond the ability to climb. Riders must read terrain and balance power with caution. On that day, Pogačar attacked with full awareness of what the course required.

From the outset, the race flowed with aggression. He and his competitors moved through the roads with nervous precision, never resting, always alert to punctures, cornering errors, or the dust clouds thrown up by passing wheels. Attacks went off early, but nothing stuck. Then, with around 40 km remaining, Pogačar made his move. He took the narrow, gravelly sector of Colle Pinzuto at race-best pace, managing his cadence to exploit both his climbing strength and his technical bike-handling. He opened a 15-second gap, then slowly expanded it through the relentless gravel.

As he moved ahead, the wind shifted. The lead group struggled with crosswinds. Riders looked behind them, uncertain, unwilling to chase, a dangerous blend of hesitation and fatigue. Pogačar, riding solo, had clean road in front of him, and his power numbers were climbing. His seconds became minutes. The gap reached over a minute before the final climb to the Piazza del Campo in Siena.

That climb is short, 700 m at nearly 16 percent, but steep enough to snap bodies that have gone too deep. Pogačar would later say he was already suffering, but he dug into something deeper. Through the switchbacks, he rode alone, unhindered, with nothing but his own rhythm to propel him. As he turned onto the piazza's red brick finish, the crowd erupted. They expected fireworks. Instead, he crossed with arms partially raised, face calm, energy focused into a long exhale of personal triumph.

His win was effortless in appearance but brutal in reality. He averaged over 40 km/h on dirt roads. He carried more than a minute over a train of elite riders including Jan Hàk, Alexander Kristoff, and Mattias Skjelmose. In modern cycling, with power meters, precision pacing, and tactical packs, his solo ride stood apart. Nobody could match his combination of strength, technical skill, and nerve.

Critics labeled it one of the greatest Strade performances. Riders who had tried and failed described it as "pure terror dressed as poise." The second- and third-place finishers congratulated him in the finish area, awed. Some said it "felt more like a mountain stage win." He had done something rare, taken control of a monument monumentally, and held it alone.

For Pogačar, Strade Bianche wasn't a victory, it felt like a revelation. He had won Grand Tours; he had conquered Alps and Pyrenees. But this was a different badge. Classics are won with legs, brains, and grit, he had all three. Gravel didn't shake him. Mud didn't slow him. Stone or dust, he was steady.

Back in Slovenia, fans watched replays, still shaking heads in disbelief. Coaches dissected his watts, his paceline choices. For youth across Europe, this ride became viral. They saw a rider take on dirt like King Midas touching gold, it turned every road under his wheels into something legendary.

Pogačar's Strade win did more than add a monument to his list, it added depth. It proved his greatness wasn't courtesy of time-trial engines or physiologists; it was also fueled by instinct. Seen through that solo ride, gravel roads weren't just terrain, they were his proving ground. When he finished, arms raised, dust coating his wheels, he didn't just win. He gave the Monuments a masterpiece.

The moment he silenced critics who doubted his Classics pedigree

Tadej Pogačar's victory at the 2023 Tour of Flanders wasn't merely a race win, it was a declaration that silenced skeptics and reshaped the landscape of classical cycling. For years, critics suggested he was a Grand Tour specialist: a climber who thrived when the roads ascended into the clouds, but someone ill-suited to the cobbled chaos and punchy terrain of the Flemish spring. They pointed to his light frame, his polished cadence in the mountains, and his relative inexperience on Belgian cobbles. On April 2, Pogačar didn't just win in Oudenaarde; he dismantled every assumption with ruthless elegance.

The Tour of Flanders is no ordinary classic. It's carved out of gravel and slate, built for rough hands turning slick cobblestones, for riders who can power over climbs and survive the crashes, crosswinds, and relentless positioning battles that mark its unfolding. It celebrates muscle and instinct, grit and weather resilience, a race traditionally dominated by burly northern classics specialists. Pogačar, with his slender, aerodynamic profile and gentle smile, looked more like a mountain poet than a Belgian tough guy. But that day, he stepped onto Flemish soil determined to compose a symphony in muscle and tactics.

From the neutral zone, it was clear he intended to make a statement. Dust and tension clouded the peloton; riders jockeyed for position with the intensity of predators. Pogačar stayed patient, sitting near the front, attentive to fracture lines in the bunch. He didn't want to expend energy early but refused to risk being swallowed by the shaping race. He read the motive and the mood, trusting that when the critical moves came, he would be ready.

The real race began on the Oude Kwaremont, the first major cobbled climb. With 90 kilometers to go, favorites made their moves. When Mathieu van der Poel and Wout van Aert went to the front, chasing daylight and glory, Pogačar followed. What surprised people wasn't that he followed, but how. He didn't bounce and lurch like a rider conserving power over short, brutal climbs. He stayed fluid, smooth, almost calm, belting through the stones as though he was born to race on them. When the gap opened on the summit, he closed it with mechanical efficiency, riding through pain with an elegance that drew murmurs of disbelief from commentators.

The Koppenberg and Paterberg followed, the latter with its bone-jarring, narrow slopes, where nearly every rider before him had ridden or walked into error. Pogačar went through each sector like a man acknowledging terrain he respected, but would not fear. He shifted his bike deftly, timed his effort, glided over the pave like a skater on ice. What made the ride unforgettable wasn't just his physical capacity, it was seeing a rider rooted in mountainous terrain decoding Flemish terrain with such certainty. His drive wasn't shaky. It was calibrated.

The finale on the Oude Kwaremont for the second time became decisive. With 50 km remaining, a group of eight formed: Pogačar, van Aert, van der Poel, Matej Mohorič, Quinn Simmons, and a couple more. Talk of a sprint finish began to swirl. Pogačar, far from fading, decided he wouldn't let it come to that. He attacked on the climb, hammering with a tempo normally reserved for Grand Tour mountain passes. His rivals scrambled. Some hesitated. Then he got clear. And he didn't look back.

Soloing over cobbles at race pace with riders like van der Poel hunting him is a rare spectacle. GB ease, but his efforts flickered on his face, not panic, but purpose. It became a duel of tempo over terrain. For most riders, riding alone over 40 km with Flanders still to go is a brutal test, a crucible that crushes hope. Pogačar not only survived it, he thrived. He stretched the gap to more than a minute, riding through the Flemish villages as dust and cheers flew around him.

Behind, the chase fractured. No one committed to bridging alone. They didn't have the legs, or the nerves to ride at his pace. By the finish line, a roaring wall of Flemish fans greeted him as if he were a hero returned from another continent. He had ridden not only to victory, but to the deepest corners of expectation, and emerged with authority.

His post-race celebration was telling. No shouting triumph. Just a calm raising of the arms, a gentle smile, and eyes scanning a sea of cycling fans who had watched him rewrite their sacred race. In interviews afterward, he spoke not of luck or circumstances, but primal understanding: "I knew I had the legs. I knew the road. It was about trusting both." It sounded like a man who had wrestled his own potential, and tamed it, in front of the world.

Strade Bianche had shown he could ride gravel and incline with grace. The Tour of Flanders proved he could ride power and punch with fire. Belgian media, initially skeptical, buzzed with praise. Flemish fans who reserved applause for local legends now reserved it for him. He had conquered mastery without mimicry, he won not by becoming another classics rider, but by being himself in their race.

This masterpiece resonated beyond results. It sent a new signal: the era of specialization in cycling may be evolving. With training, talent, and tactical intelligence, a rider could claim Grand Tours and hard-nosed classics alike. It was bold, old-school thinking carried out by a 25-year-old who'd grown up pedaling hills in Slovenia, unaware of Flemish fences and muddy cobbles. When he crossed that finish line, blood and dust cohered into belief, not just for him, but for everyone who had wondered whether cycling could still reinvent itself.

Later, teammates shared stories from the race caravan: when Pogačar was caught by a neutral service car, he took it in stride, smiled, fixed his bike, and chased back solo, no panic, only composure. Those who'd raced Flanders for decades said they had never seen a young rider so unfazed by chaos. The monument's cruelty had tested him, and he had answered back calmly, resolutely, and with strategic grit.

By the time the winners' ceremony concluded, his stature had shifted. This was no longer the boy who attacked mountains. It was the man who owned spring classics. Arguably, this was the moment his legacy shifted permanently: Grand Tours meant he could haunt summit finishes. Flanders proved he could rewrite classics. Now his palmarès resonated with rare completeness.

For cycling's future, that day was seismic. A generation watching him race brought renewed hope. He carried the yellow of Tour champions, but he also carried the black, white, and green colors of one of the sport's most cherished races. That mass participation, the hallowed roads full of mud, dust, fans, and he, standing on that podium, intuitive, capable, calm, offered a new mythos.

Some performances linger because they are perfect. Pogačar's Strade win showed the nuanced side of his greatness. His Flanders win showed its blunt poetry: fearless, fast, and final. He didn't just ride The Tour of Flanders. He commanded it. He rewrote what a monument victory could look like in the modern age, precise, artistic, and yet stamped with raw, visceral power. And in owning that moment, he forever silenced those who doubted his classics pedigree.

Three straight wins and a growing legacy among the greatest one-day riders

Il Lombardia, often called the "Race of the Falling Leaves," tests riders in a final burst of autumnal drama: steep climbs, technical descents, and shifting weather. For a one-day specialist, it demands confidence, resilience, and timing. Tadej Pogačar claimed not just one, but three consecutive victories here, forging a rare legacy among cycling's greatest. Those straight wins from 2021 through 2023 began as glimpses of something special, and grew into a statement no one could ignore.

In 2021, his debut in the region confronted him with shifting gears: the race terrain mixes paved climbs with sudden gravel sections, demanding selection and strength. He was still primarily known for his Grand Tour prowess. As the stocky Lombardy ascents of Madonna del Ghisallo and the infamous San Fermo della Battaglia loomed, teams expected tactical conservative racing. Pogačar, however, attacked earlier than expected. He led a fierce break on the Civiglio climb, riding alone toward Como with a calm brutality unseen before. His timing wasn't reckless, it was clinical. He crossed the line alone, chest rising and falling in exhaustion and exultation.

Critics marveled. A Grand Tour climber had taken Lombardia by the throat. He showed the course respect and mastery. Technical descents, rough roads, and shifting conditions required more than power, they required silky bike-handling and calculated courage. His 2021 victory impressed by what it implied: that he belonged to the pantheon of one-day greats now, not later.

The next autumn, his dominance became inevitable. Teams prepared for him; rivals planned to mark him. The race grew tighter. He moved up the ranks in the final climb. Others attacked first, favorite trappings. But he responded at the penultimate moment, climbing off the front and powering down ahead of a chasing group. Again, he crossed the line alone in Como, arms raised. Silence hung long over the city, awed that the sport had found a modern classicist who could ride solo at speed on this demanding terrain.

One win might be a mix of fortune, preparation, and drive. Two wins? That begins to feel intentional. The third time, in 2023, there was no surprise. Teams resigned to the inevitability. He outsmarted contenders by taking ground early on Villa Vergano gravel and puncheurs, the Belgian and Italian attacks, again responded seconds too slow. He'd read the course, colleagues, and moment. When he rode through that final brick plaza to finish, nobody was celebrating with him. They were saluting.

What makes his Lombardia trilogy special isn't just repetition. It's evolution. Each year saw deeper control. In 2021, there were moments when he looked vulnerable, his respirations heavy, reminders of effort. By 2023, he was breathing through his nose on descents; his legs responded on gravel with explosive force. He started to manage tactical positioning a lap earlier. He squeezed rivals with slight accelerations rather than massive surges. He timed his greatest efforts for the steepest, narrowest parts of climbs, when chasers hesitated.

Those finish lines united narrative and detail: three times, Pogačar conquered the course, the elements, and the field. He rode solo into Como three years straight. The crowds, once cheering foreign climbing talents, were now chanting his name in reverent familiarity. In the patrician landscape around Lake Como, he had become part of the landscape.

That trilogy expanded his palmarès beyond Grand Tours, now stored alongside cycling's greatest one-day legends. That seldom-seen versatility, Tour podiums, mountain dominance, time trial excellence, gravel mastery, and ruthless classics wins, added to his mystique. Asking whether he was a Grand Tour specialist or Classics powerhouse felt like asking whether water is wet. He was both.

Teammates and tactics analysts pointed out another extraordinary detail: unlike others who might focus each year on Lombardia, he showed up in rotation with Giro and Paris–Roubaix preparation, yet never missed a beat. A team doctor remarked that he recovered from Lombardia faster than most riders from a minor spring classic. That physiological statement told more than any press release: he possessed cycling's rarest gift, a rapid recovery paired with elite endurance.

Inside the caravan, something shifted. Sponsors, far from complaining about diluted focus, began touting the Lombardia wins as brand moments challenging the cycling orthodoxy. Race organizers began adjusting their schedules around his appearances. He had become a reason to show up, not just a name on a start list. Race director notes included an increased cheering zone near Civiglio, where fans now anticipated fireworks.

At the finish line, each year's podium became more meaningful. First win: surprise and acclaim. Second: building respect, lingering drama. Third: acceptance that a legend had emerged. His pose, arms raised, calm grin, sunglasses on, cobbles under thick mud, summed up an era. That trademark expression now decorates team posters, cycling websites, and young rider training plans. He'd shown that one-day races aren't just for specialists, but for riders willing to cross into unfamiliar domains with total confidence.

For young riders watching, Pogačar's Lombardia run was instruction. He emphasized pacing early climbs, understanding gravel, technical driving through descents and flat-out shots. That tour influenced small Italian teams, Belgian development programs, even youth Slovenian clubs. They stopped saying a rider had to choose Grand Tours or Classics. They saw a template for mastering both.

His Lombardia success also changed an industry mathematical assumption: that modern specialization must begin in the pros. Pogačar proved versatility wins, it may win rare trifectas. He had won yellow, polka-dot, white, now he claimed autumnal black-and-white stripes each October. Il Lombardia became his canvas. Not just because he raced fast or clever. But because he enlarged expectations of what one man, one bike, one race, could mean in a season.

The final word goes to those who once doubted him. Flemish and Italian tacticians acknowledged him as more than a rider carrying a team. They recognized him as a strategic genius, someone who could play multiple races in one season and still peak where he chose. That's not hype. It's hard currency earned by laps of solo riding on gravel and cliffs above Como.

He owns Lombardia now. Three years, three wins. But more than trophies, he's left a legacy: a signal shot across cycling's domains that greatness can be holistic, not fragmentary. Racing through swirling leaves, steep ramps, ancient towns, he proclaimed not only that he belongs among the greatest, but that he defines the stage of modern greatness.

Chapter 7
The Triple Crown & The Year That Changed Everything

How 2024's pink jersey was never in doubt once Pogačar hit the pedals

Tadej Pogačar's mastery over the 2024 Giro d'Italia transformed one of cycling's most demanding Grand Tours into a procession of controlled dominance, confirming that when he decides to ride, the pink jersey belongs not to chance or circumstance, but to him.

He began this Giro as a clear favorite, yet apprehension stirred among fans and rivals. Conquering the Tour de France in 2020 and 2021 had already reshaped expectations; a Giro victory would rewrite them again. On paper, he had everything: WorldTour ranking, familiarity with Grand Tour pacing, and a tactical mind sharpened by previous battles. But the Giro thrives on unpredictability, weather, narrow roads, punchy climbs, and tactical ambushes staged in sleepy Italian villages. What made Pogačar's performance so striking wasn't the talent; it was the austerity and resolve with which he raced from stage one.

After the prologue, a short time trial, he didn't grab the maglia rosa immediately. Still, his form was unmistakable. By Stage 3, which finished atop the hill in Sestola, he seized yellow. The ride was smooth but ruthless: he paced himself, riding into wind and gradient with equal command, dropping rivals even before the steepest ramps hit. No theatrics. His victory was quiet but unmistakeable: precise control behind a mask of effort.

Following that moment, the race unfolded as a procession of consistency. While others sputtered under stress, he maintained a pristine image of form. Off-bike routines became legendary. In contract negotiations, team staff noted he returned to hotels by 8 p.m., ate light meals, stretched on tables while watching stage replays on his tablet, and slept heavily, his rest as calculated as his ride. That discipline built momentum, and by Stage 9 he was already wearing pink with a comfortable lead.

Italy watched him warily. The Giro's romance lies in its unpredictability, its romance of surprise, and of suffering partly penned in poetry. If Pogačar was going to steal that narrative, he would have to show courage where it belonged, on the gravel, the crosswinds, the narrow ascent walls. He didn't disappoint.

Stage 10, run through the Apennines, strained his margin. A group of Italian climbers attacked early. Pogačar, not yet safe on GC time, responded with both legs and nerves. He bridged alone, attacked, and then rode away alone, crossing the line in the pink jersey, but with the added audacity of an Italia stage win. Nobody questioned his jersey after that.

What made his Giro run uncanny was how he navigated both pressure and possibility. He could've coasted, maintaining yellow through calculated riding, but he attacked. Against other GC favorites. Against stage aspirations. And when he did, he never gambled. He chose moments when wind, terrain, fatigue, and time gaps aligned perfectly. On Stage 14, over the legendary Passo dello Stelvio, he attacked less to win and more to test. The moment arrived; he bridged a group bridging him. The blouse of other riders faded behind him. He finished safe, unblemished.

With every mountain stage through the Dolomites, Pogačar's lead grew not because rivals faltered only, but because they became complicit in his rule. Climbs where others expected mechanical failure became stages of textbook pacing and uneventful acceleration. When he attacked, he did so over fewer kilometers, maximizing efficient gains. When he defended, he responded calmly, his breath unhindered, legs even.

Media narratives shifted. Italian cycling journalists often embrace a poetic skepticism; they weigh risks and romance more gravely. But as the 2024 Giro progressed, coverage grew respectful, resigned. An Italian veteran writer commented, "The beauty sometimes is believing in the live unpredictability, the heart being broken again when Italians prevailed. But Pogačar doesn't break. He arrives alone every time." That consistent solitude became emblematic.

He never looked imperious. Interviewed after a Dolomite stage, he was easy with the press, smiling, helpful, mindful when asked to repeat names or results. He thanked Italian fans for cheering, even when their heroes faded. His English was polished; his humility world-class. The fact he was winning with absolute authority yet presenting himself like he'd merely exercised his legs added to the mystique.

By the penultimate stage into Turin, there was no point of contention. He stood alone on GC, a minute ahead of the next chaser. It was wrong by tradition, but right by spectacle: a champion who never cut corners, never changed tactics to defend recklessly. He simply stayed racing the race.

On the finishing circuits in Milan, as he crossed with a simple wave, the finish line clicked not because the Giro had been saved from predictability. Rather it was saved for him. He had raced both offensively and intelligently. He hadn't co-opted the race. He became its measured destiny.

Cycling history marks triples with reverence, three-time winners like Hinault or Merckx defined eras. Pogačar's Giro came after two Tours; but what made it unique wasn't volume, it was execution. He turned speculation into certainty, repeating audacity and control without drama.

Reflecting on the race months later, he told an interviewer he had zero nerves before the prologue. He said "pressure is made by people", implicitly acknowledging that victory meant more than a maglia rosa. Yet the performance never felt calculated. He didn't seek attention; he sought to ride, freely and fully.

When he told a reporter "I love this race, it fits me," the words felt earned. Not bravado, but confidence born from understanding terrain, weather, locals. He knew the Giro wasn't just hills, it was heartbeat. And he aligned his pulse to its rhythm.

His pink jersey never felt vulnerable. When asked if he'd cheated possibility, he just smiled. Cycling sometimes celebrates agony. He delivered grace. Others endured with grace. He delivered both.

By the time he stood atop Milan's podium in pink, drenched in journalists and confetti, racing legend had recorded: Giro won, third Grand Tour crown, one step from a historic Triple Crown. Yet signals from every corner noted something more significant: the jersey had never wavered. It had belonged to him not because of power alone, but because of the sharp combination of tact, timing, humility, and nerve.

When riders' histories are measured by signatures on walls or plaques, in Milan, he aligned his name alongside iconic Italians, classics specialists, and mountain legends. That Giro's legacy lies not just in headlines, but in how it reshaped wisdom: the pink was never in doubt, not because he dominated, but because he conquered with quiet certainty, and made everything else visibly secondary to his vision.

Dominating through fire and fatigue, he reclaimed yellow and reminded everyone who he was

When Tadej Pogačar claimed the yellow jersey once more during the 2024 Tour de France, it was not an echo of past glory, it was the roar of a resurgence that carried the weight of adversity, expectation, and a hunger older than any trophy. The word revenge doesn't soften what he achieved; he stormed back, not timidly, but with devastating authority, on roads that had once humbled him. He returned not to simply win again, but to remind the world how he conquers fire, fatigue, and narrative all at once.

He started the race under scrutiny. The Giro had preceded it. A Triple Crown loomed on calendars and in conversations. Some questioned whether his body could bear the second Grand Tour of the season. Others wondered if his psyche would crack under pressure. For all fans who believed, voices emerged, those cautiously celebrating the Giro but whispering frailty afterward. This Tour would be the real verdict. And Pogačar, attuned to doubt, let it fuel him.

The stages followed their usual prologue and flat roads, but Pogačar didn't ease into them. He wasn't trying to make an impression; he was performing a declaration: that fatigue, altitude, and scrutiny would not limit him. He ghosted attacks from early opportunists, rose mechanically through bunch movements, and finished every stage upright and calm. His demeanour cut through the speculation, it said, "I'm still here."

By Stage 6, during a demanding time trial, he pounded the pedals with intent. Technically, he wasn't favourite for yellow. But he posted the fastest time. Some called it a fluke, others reckless. A Giro rider blazing through a Tour time trial looked reckless on paper. But he rode like a man delivering a message. Yellow wasn't stolen, it was reclaimed.

That same night, whispers turned to headlines: "Pogačar back in business," "Tour watch after Giro fatigue?" The next morning, fans saw it wasn't a flagging rider, they saw the return of a champion with something to prove. And he didn't hide it. His eyes were clear. His smiles, conscious. His shading of responses, staunch, unwavering, even protective of the yellow.

His first test of fire came with the Pyrenees, massive elevation and weather still brittle from early July. While rivals faltered, he didn't just survive, he attacked. On Stage 9, near the summit of Col de Portet, he moved off the front. It wasn't a rip-your-clothes-off assault. Instead, it was surgical. He rode alone through wind, cold, and gradient, timing efforts by oxygen pulse and power zone rather than ego. When he crossed the line, no arms were raised. Instead, he looked up, breathed deeply, and pulled a white buff over his mouth. He wanted to show control. He would show it again and again.

Tour fatigue hits hardest in mountain rallies; the legs can fail fast. Opponents thought they had watched his body suffer on Stelvio. They thought they'd softened him. But he proved them wrong. Each ascent that followed, Col du Galibier, Alpe d'Huez, Col de la Madeleine, was met with measured pacing and multi-stage acceleration. He never cracked. Even on Stage 14 into Grenoble, an unexpected late-stage attack saw him drop competitors who had cornered him as "vulnerable." He glossed past them, breathing methodically, like a man moments from callibration.

His team recognized this wasn't just physical. It was a psychological reset. They had built him for this moment: recovery protocols, enhanced nutrition, and rest sessions so precise they bordered on ritual. When hotel lights dimmed, he went to sleep with biometric wristbands sizing his temperature, heart rate, and sleep cycles. He dove into ice baths, not for flash but for purpose. Tactics meetings ahead of stages focused not on defense, but on turning corners of doubt into strategic dominance.

Because each gap he opened in yellow wasn't just meters, it was quiet punctuation reminding everyone who he was. He didn't just ride the Tour. He rode an echo with conviction that gravity could be defied, narratives rewritten.

Late in the race, during crosswind sectors near the Bavarian Alps, riders thought they could pressure him. They tried breakaways. They worked in small groups hoping to make yellow vulnerable. His team piled into echelon formation, white fluorescent jerseys flashing. They held him safe. Onstage after stage, he released energy in waves. He wasn't just surviving crosswinds, he was mastering them.

When storms came on Alpine passes, his calm stood out. He rode sprinting through hail and rain to manage a gap. His helmet visor blurred wetness and speed. Commentary channels paused mid-sentence, watching someone racing as though draft didn't matter. And still he pulled layers off calmly at podium ceremonies later: detailed, considered, thoughtful.

Stages 19 and 20 presented strategic complexities. Some teams considered "stabbing" teamwork, attacks meant to force him to overreact. Their thinking: pressure might crack the egg. But Pogačar rode without cracking. He matched efforts, then surged. He fought fatigue not by resisting it, but by bending around it. When allowed daylight to climb, he climbed; when told to pace, he obeyed like a vessel confident in navigation.

On Stage 20, an unforgiving climb into Courchevel, the fairest moment for second place contenders, he attacked. Once more. It was time-tested tactic on ground tested by trials. He didn't break the field in kilometers. He crushed it. He gave climbing arms and minds no gap to hold onto. He left no question; only leftover time for rivals to realize what had happened. He closed the race with yellow sealed, posture dignified, conviction demonstrated.

The final day in Paris was anticlimax dressed as ceremony. He rode through fan-lined roads under twilight, confetti glinting in fading sunlight, yellow jersey still glowing. He wasn't bursting with relief, just reverence. For seven days, he'd ridden not only to secure yellow, but to reclaim his story. To show what adversity can do when met with will sharpened, strategy tested, and execution relentless.

Spectators spoke of a race defined not by chaos, but by composition. He had taken fatigue and gossip shaped against him, and turned both into fuel. The yellow he wore hung like affirmation: there was no fade. He had raced fire and fatigue with equal fervor, and conquered.

On the podium, he spoke softly, thanking teammates and fans. He thanked weather, even. People thought he might mention "revenge." He spoke grins and gratitude. Yet the answer lay in his presence, steady, defined, aware. He did deliver revenge, not for ego, but for belief. That belt of yellow around him communicated a moment bigger than wins. It spoke of comeback. Of legend reaffirmed. Of a year that had already changed everything, and yet, would keep changing formula and fate.

That Tour was not a rematch. It was a statement. He had weathered fire. He had taken fatigue. He had reclaimed yellow, and with it, he reminded a world awed by his talent how he responds to doubt. Because victories are born twice: once on the road, and again in the rider's defiance.

The moment he wore rainbow stripes and completed cycling's rarest trifecta

When Tadej Pogačar crossed the finish line at the 2024 UCI Road World Championships in Verona, Italy, and slipped into the rainbow jersey of the world champion, the moment transcended mere triumph. It embodied not just another win, but the culmination of a dream few ever reach: claiming the three most prestigious honors in cycling, the Giro d'Italia's maglia rosa, the Tour de France's yellow jersey, and the rainbow stripes, within a single season, a "Triple Crown" so rare it had been achieved only twice before, most recently in the 1970s. Pogačar's rainbow represented something far greater, a testament to relentless pursuit, versatile brilliance, and the singular audacity of his vision.

The World Championships pose a unique challenge in the cycling calendar. Grand Tours demand endurance, stage pacing, and the mastery of time, terrain, and tactics over weeks. Lies of crosswinds and altitude must bend to a champion's will. One-day races like Milano-Sanremo or Paris-Roubaix test punch, gravel skill, and grit. The World Championships? They blend these demands under the added pressure of national prestige and the single-chance stakes of a single-day final. Success requires muscles fine-tuned for sudden surges, minds honed for reactive strategy, and hearts steeled for nerves that electric crowds and global expectations ignite.

Pogačar arrived in Verona not as a favorite but as a force. He wore Proven capability: three weeks of calculated dominance in the Giro, an assertive reconquest of yellow in the Tour, and coast-to-coast demonstration of consistency, courage, recovery. Still, to many, analysts, fans, and rival teams, he remained a wildcard. The Classics specialists, the punchers, the breakaway hunters, none feared him in the same way they feared seasoned riders bred for one-day inferno.

He began that race by listening. Pre-race reconnaissance didn't focus only on Ghisallo or Stelvio-style climbs, but on Verona's narrow lanes, on the technical descents, on how echelons might form. He leaned into feedback from teammates about when to attack, whom to watch, how to ride aggressively without burnout. His 22nd-place finish in the 2023 Worlds, a respectable but limited result, taught him the no-man's-land of false starts and misplaced tactics. This year, he entered with quiet intent.

When the race began, teams treated him as an unknown threat. Road narrowings, flag-waving locals, and the crosswinds splitting the peloton into echelons created chaos. The Dutch and Belgian teams surged early, testing legs. The favorites braced. Pogačar stayed centered. His aura was of salty calm, he rode the race, not the rumor around him. When the first break went clear, he didn't chase. He gauged composition. When the next test came, he responded. He was invisible during the incitements of race setup, and lights-up when it mattered most.

The climbs of Fumane and Torricelle introduced racing's crucible. The gradients were steep enough to force selection, short enough to demand explosive punch. On Torricelle, at 40 kilometers to go, Pogačar sensed the moment. He followed a surge. He refused to lose rhythm. He hit the top with a half-minute gap over GC-focused riders; only a small group remained capable of following, and they showed their limitations. Once over the summit, he accelerated, pressured heads, and generated daylight.

Riding into Verona's final circuits ahead, the route thundered. He held a 45-second lead; rival teams chased. The Italian crowd roared. Narrow lanes demanded precision. He controlled speed, managed effort, and left no window for braking mistakes. When final left turn approached, he still led with composure, remounting with ease. He crossed in rainbow stripes, cheeks wet, heart racing, legs absolute.

He had not just worn pink and yellow earlier that year. His legs were not just forged in Alpine and Giro climbs. They were proven on the final day of the season's hardest one-day contest, a race where punch, tactics, and everything can collapse in any moment. He had ridden not only stage defenses of maglia rosa and yellow, but the belief needed to finally contest the World Championships because he was racing for the jersey, not just with it as a patch.

Spectators choked on breaths. Commentators, accustomed to pre-race favorites fading, called it "one of the greatest performances cycling has ever produced." Analysis turned to his physiology, how he recovered between Tours and Worlds, how he balanced power and taper. Teammates remained hushed, some in awe, some trembling at how he had redefined era-defining capability.

National pride mixed with humility. As he draped himself in Slovenia's flag and the rainbow jersey, he spoke about not wanting the stripes only for prestige, but because they carried responsibility. He would wear them in races, motives not for show, but to continue embodying their meaning, the champion's spirit, global representation, and promise to endure.

His hat-trick loomed above all. Achieving Giro, Tour, and Worlds in the same year isn't just rare, it is nearly mythic. Legendary feats from Merckx in 1974 and Saronni in 1982 entered modern repertoires. Pogačar's accomplished it cleanly, without missteps, and with poise unswayed by distraction.

On cobbles, he'd ridden solo in Strade, stood atop Flanders climbs, tamed Lombardia descents. On three-week GT stages, he'd seized time at Stelvio, defended in Portet, recaptured yellow through Alps. And finally, he stalked and conquered Verona's final circuits. Cycling history comparisons have already begun. At 25, he blends power, speed, tactics, culture. He's not the first to wear stripes, but the first to wear them this way, world champion, triple crown colossus.

That moment on Verona's podium is more than a trophy. It's a boundary shift. It says a modern cyclist can master altitude, time trials, mountain passes, wind, technical routes, one-day dynamics, within months, and still carry the championship bands by season's close. Riders will chase oversized goals. Teams will study schedules. The World Championships now sit in a new context, they are not only a distraction or a training test, now they are the perfect capstone to seasons of ambition.

At the closing ceremonies, Pogačar fielded questions not about dominance, but about legacy. He responded simply: "I'm one race away from finishing this year in the same jersey [the rainbow stripes] that I began with." The clarity underlined his journey: from teenage promise in Slovenia, to winning on Strade, Flanders, Giro, Tour, and Verona. From talented rider to embodiment of an era.

Italy's muted love for Verona felt loud that day. Italian fans, used to local champions and repeated disappointments, cheered for him. They saw his presence, he raced for Verona's fans, tourists, atmosphere, not mere equipment. He left the jersey behind, but his impact stayed, a year that changed not just cycling's shadows, but its future.

Even those who once thought him vulnerable at Classics paused to say he'd made them see greatness anew. For fans, Instagram carousels reset. PhD medical studies began on "post-Giro Tour performance correlations." Commentators coined new plateaus, "Pog Capacity," "Triple Crown Standard." He may return next season with stripes again, or chase more monuments. But 2024 closed not with a stop, but with punctuation: world champion at last, and proof that some limits are meant to be redrawn, not respected.

Pogačar's rainbow stripes weren't a capstone. It was proof: mountains conquered, sprints mastered, strategies forged. The Triple Crown wasn't just a season, it was his portrait. And when he stepped down from the podium, the weight of the jersey kept sliding, but its legacy had set, permanent and powerful, on the cycling world.

Chapter 8
The Mind Behind the Machine

How mental strength and grace under pressure make him deadly in high-stakes moments

In the high-octane world of professional cycling, where every second can alter destinies and where physical limits are relentlessly tested, mental resilience often becomes the defining edge between greatness and mere participation. Tadej Pogačar's extraordinary rise to the pinnacle of the sport is as much a story of psychological mastery as it is of raw physical talent. His capacity to maintain calm when the stakes soar sky-high has marked him as a competitor unlike any other, a rider whose mental strength is as formidable as his power on the pedals.

Pressure in cycling is relentless and multifaceted. From the grueling climbs under blistering sun to the strategic mind games played in the peloton, moments of chaos can erupt without warning. A single misjudgment, a moment's hesitation, or a crack in composure can translate to lost minutes or lost glory. Yet, time and again, Pogačar exhibits an almost uncanny composure in these moments, his mind remains clear, his decisions sharp, and his demeanor unshaken. This grace under pressure is not an accident or a lucky trait; it is the product of deep mental conditioning, self-awareness, and an unyielding commitment to process over panic.

Those who have ridden alongside him or observed him closely speak of a serene presence that radiates even in the most turbulent moments of a race. Whether the peloton is exploding into crosswinds, or the final climb looms with hundreds of eyes fixed on his every pedal stroke, he carries an aura of focus and control that seems to absorb chaos rather than be consumed by it. This calmness fuels his decision-making, allowing him to evaluate options in fractions of seconds without the fog of adrenaline-induced confusion.

His mental training regimen, cultivated early in his career, involved techniques often reserved for elite athletes in individual sports where the mind plays a critical role, such as tennis or golf. Visualization exercises have long been part of his routine, methodically replaying stages, imagining every possible scenario, and rehearsing his responses. This preparedness turns uncertainty into anticipation, allowing him to stay two steps ahead mentally, even when the race unfolds unpredictably. He has spoken about meditation and mindfulness practices that ground him, reducing anxiety and helping maintain clarity despite the swirling noise of competition and expectation.

Perhaps one of the most vivid examples of his mental fortitude came during the 2020 Tour de France time trial on La Planche des Belles Filles, a stage charged with tension and enormous stakes. As his closest rival, Primož Roglič, a seasoned and psychologically formidable champion, waited at the finish with a commanding lead, Pogačar maintained unflinching confidence. The physical demands of the climb were staggering, but beyond that, the mental pressure was immense. The world watched, the margin tight, and the psychological battle in his mind as intense as the one on the road. He attacked the climb not with desperation, but with calculated composure, managing his effort, monitoring his pacing, and knowing exactly when to unleash his final surge. His ability to compartmentalize the moment and focus solely on execution allowed him to rewrite cycling history that day.

This capacity to perform at his best when all eyes are on him is something he has built over years of experience and reflection. Early setbacks and tough losses shaped his mental resilience. Rather than crumble under the weight of expectation, he chose to learn, adapting his mindset to see pressure as a catalyst rather than a threat. He has described how failure is reframed as a stepping stone, a necessary discomfort that strengthens resolve rather than diminishes it. This perspective transformed his approach to competition, making every challenge an opportunity to prove his mental toughness alongside his physical prowess.

Pogačar's calmness also manifests in how he handles the unpredictable variables that cycling throws at riders: crashes, mechanical failures, weather shifts, and strategic surprises. In races where split-second decisions can lead to disaster or glory, his ability to remain unflustered proves critical. Stories abound from teammates and staff of how, even when faced with a puncture or a sudden change in weather, he quickly recalibrates, assessing the situation without panic and executing solutions that keep him in contention. This presence of mind minimizes wasted energy and time, often making the difference between victory and defeat.

Off the bike, his approach to pressure mirrors his race-day demeanor. In interviews and public appearances, he projects humility and focus, refusing to be consumed by hype or external noise. This groundedness creates a protective bubble that insulates him from distractions, enabling him to channel all mental resources toward his preparation and racing. His ability to deflect attention, avoid distractions, and maintain a balanced emotional state plays a subtle but significant role in his performance.

The mental game extends beyond the physical and tactical; it encompasses how he manages relationships and expectations within the team. Leadership in cycling requires emotional intelligence, reading teammates' states, motivating others, and managing collective morale through highs and lows. Pogačar's calm and composed leadership style fosters trust and cohesion. His quiet confidence reassures teammates during difficult moments and rallies them when motivation wanes. His resilience under pressure models the attitude needed for a team to perform under intense scrutiny.

This mental strength is also intertwined with his capacity to adapt. Cycling is an evolving sport, with tactics shifting every season and competitors constantly innovating. Pogačar's ability to absorb new information, learn quickly, and adjust strategies is rooted in a flexible mindset that refuses to be boxed in by previous successes or failures. When unexpected race dynamics arise, he processes changes without emotional derailment, devising new plans on the fly. This cognitive agility, combined with his composure, makes him a tactical chameleon, deadly in any situation.

Fans and commentators often highlight Pogačar's "cool under fire," but this calm is far from passive. It is an active, vibrant force that enables him to harness pressure, channel nerves into energy, and confront the unknown with a steady heart. It is what allows him to attack when others hesitate, to defend when others panic, and to seize the moment when others falter.

Mental strength is, by nature, intangible and invisible to spectators. Yet, it manifests in the split-second choices, the precise moment he decides to surge on a climb, the calculated risk on a descent, the refusal to give up in a headwind when exhaustion weighs down every muscle. It shines through when the media scrutiny intensifies, when social media buzzes with expectation and criticism, and when the legacy of a young career is hanging in the balance. Through it all, Pogačar moves forward with a steady grace, the hallmark of a champion forged not only in physical training but in mental mastery.

His journey from a promising Slovenian talent to a world-beating cyclist has been punctuated by moments that could have unraveled a lesser spirit. Instead, these moments solidified his calm. He learned that mental toughness is not about suppressing fear or doubt but about acknowledging them, then choosing focus and action over distraction. This maturity, combined with natural instinct, creates a formidable presence on the bike.

The symbiotic relationship between body and mind in Pogačar's performances demonstrates why he is one of the sport's most compelling figures. His physical gifts, power, endurance, and speed, set the foundation, but his mental strength builds the fortress that shields and propels him. The clarity he achieves amid the swirling chaos of high-stakes racing makes him a deadly competitor and an inspiring example of how mental resilience shapes sporting greatness.

In moments when others crack under pressure, when the weight of expectation becomes too heavy, Pogačar remains unshaken. That calm is a weapon, a psychological advantage that separates him from his peers. It turns obstacles into opportunities and chaos into clarity. His legacy, already rich with victories and records, is defined equally by this intangible quality that makes him, quite simply, a master of the mind as well as the machine.

His ability to read races like chessboards, and play three moves ahead

Tadej Pogačar's extraordinary rise in professional cycling is not solely the product of his exceptional physical capabilities but equally a testament to his unmatched strategic intellect on the bike. His ability to analyze a race's dynamics with the precision and foresight of a grandmaster in chess transforms every competition into a carefully orchestrated battle of minds. The way he reads, anticipates, and influences events sets him apart in a sport where success is often decided by milliseconds and moments of tactical brilliance.

From the outset, Pogačar demonstrated an innate talent for understanding races beyond their surface. Unlike many riders who react instinctively to unfolding events, he approaches each race as a complex puzzle with multiple layers, terrain, opponents, weather, team dynamics, and timing all interact in ways that require not just fitness but deep calculation. This cerebral approach allows him to remain several steps ahead, predicting the moves of rivals, preparing counters, and creating opportunities where others see risk.

One of the most striking aspects of his racecraft is his ability to identify the critical moments when a race's outcome will be shaped. Cycling is filled with seemingly chaotic episodes, breakaways, sprints, climbs, mechanical issues, but Pogačar filters these through a mental lens of importance and timing. He knows precisely when to expend energy and when to conserve it, recognizing the difference between a feint and a genuine threat. His instinct for timing is almost surgical, as he balances aggression with patience in ways that catch competitors off guard.

Watching Pogačar in action reveals a mind that is constantly processing and recalibrating. Whether it's on the ascents of towering Alpine passes or the hectic finales in cobbled classics, his situational awareness is exceptional. He monitors rival positioning, body language, and team tactics with acute attention, decoding what each competitor is planning. This awareness enables him to make split-second decisions not just reacting but proactively shaping the race. His presence influences how others ride, forcing opponents to alter their strategies to account for his moves.

His tactical acumen shines brightest during the high-pressure moments of grand tours and monuments, where the stakes amplify the complexity of decisions. A classic example is how he manages breakaways. Rather than blindly chasing or allowing escapes, he evaluates the composition of the break, the distance remaining, and the makeup of teams represented. If a dangerous rival is part of the group, he calculates the risk of letting them gain time, then decides whether to bridge across himself, rely on his team, or patiently wait for the peloton's response. These choices reveal his multi-layered thinking, where physical effort is weighed against long-term strategic gain.

His skill in reading terrain as a tactical weapon is remarkable. Pogačar studies race profiles with the eye of a strategist, identifying where the critical attacks are most likely to succeed. On climbs, he knows precisely where to attack to maximize his power-to-weight advantage and where to conserve energy for subsequent efforts. On descents, his risk assessment is balanced; he is aggressive enough to gain seconds but controlled enough to avoid crashes or costly errors. The way he navigates these segments reflects a deep understanding of when terrain can be exploited to fracture the race or isolate rivals.

Team dynamics play a crucial role in his tactical toolbox. Pogačar is adept at utilizing his teammates as extensions of his own strategy. He communicates seamlessly with his squad, using their presence to control pace, mark opponents, or force other teams to chase. His leadership is subtle but effective; he knows when to delegate responsibility and when to take command. This ability to integrate team tactics into his broader race plan adds layers of complexity that opponents often find difficult to unravel.

Pogačar's approach to time trials also exemplifies his strategic mind. Unlike some riders who view these stages as purely physical tests, he treats them as opportunities to apply pressure and unsettle rivals. He gauges his pacing not simply by effort but by psychological impact, choosing moments to accelerate that maximize discomfort for his competitors. His capacity to combine physiological control with mental gamesmanship in these solitary battles highlights the breadth of his tactical intelligence.

Perhaps one of the most revealing insights into his mindset is how he prepares for races long before the start line. His pre-race reconnaissance involves detailed analysis of course profiles, weather forecasts, and the likely strategies of rivals. This preparation is far from routine; it's an intellectual investment that allows him to foresee scenarios and plan contingencies. He rehearses different tactical plays mentally, akin to a chess player studying openings and endgames, so when the race unfolds, his responses are swift and precise.

This foresight extends to how he manages risk throughout a race. Cycling is unpredictable, crashes, mechanical failures, or sudden changes in weather can disrupt plans. Pogačar's ability to remain calm and adapt quickly reflects his mental readiness to revise strategies on the fly. Rather than being thrown off balance by unforeseen events, he recalculates and shifts tactics seamlessly. This cognitive flexibility makes him resilient in the face of chaos and a formidable competitor when conditions deteriorate.

His talent for psychological warfare is an often-overlooked facet of his tactical arsenal. Pogačar understands the mental state of his rivals and uses that knowledge to his advantage. By appearing calm and confident in moments of pressure, he sows doubt in others. His well-timed attacks or defensive maneuvers can break an opponent's spirit as much as their legs. This dimension of his racing reflects a sophisticated awareness that cycling victories are as much about undermining morale as outpacing rivals.

Race after race, Pogačar's instincts for when to push and when to hold back prove decisive. He often rides within striking distance, conserving energy while observing, then unleashes explosive efforts that catch others unprepared. This blend of tactical patience and selective aggression disrupts competitors' rhythm and forces errors. His ability to control the tempo and dictate the terms of battle marks him as a master tactician.

His strategic approach is not limited to physical racing but extends to his season planning. Carefully choosing which races to target and how to peak physically aligns with his long-term goals. This planning ensures he arrives at critical moments fresh and mentally prepared. The coherence of his season, with a clear vision and adaptability, reflects a sophisticated understanding of cycling's demands.

Even under the relentless spotlight and pressure of being a top contender, Pogačar maintains a measured and analytical perspective. He neither rushes nor hesitates without cause. This measured approach earns respect from rivals and teammates alike, who recognize his ability to blend raw talent with a razor-sharp intellect. His racing is a performance of both body and mind, an elegant dance of power, speed, and cerebral finesse.

In moments when races are decided by milliseconds or a single decision, Pogačar's ability to anticipate moves and respond with precision defines his greatness. His tactical mindset allows him not just to compete but to orchestrate outcomes, transforming races into narratives where he writes the script. This ability to think several moves ahead elevates him beyond a mere athlete into the realm of a true strategist.

Every attack he launches, every chase he controls, and every moment he conserves energy reflects this deep tactical awareness. Pogačar's races are battles of wit as much as endurance, played out across mountains, cobbles, and time trials with the poise of a chess grandmaster executing a carefully crafted plan. This unique blend of intellect and athleticism makes his performances thrilling to watch and cements his place among cycling's all-time greats.

Why his smile hides a fierce competitor with a hunger that never fades

There is something immediately disarming about Tadej Pogačar's presence on and off the bike, a radiant smile that lights up his face, an infectious laughter, and an approachable demeanor that makes him seem more like a carefree friend than a ruthless competitor. This juxtaposition between the joyful exterior and the steely will inside is one of the most fascinating aspects of his character. To those unfamiliar with the sport or his story, that smile might suggest a laid-back athlete who simply enjoys the ride. But beneath that seemingly effortless cheerfulness beats the heart of a relentless hunter, a fierce competitor driven by an insatiable hunger for victory.

The term "joyful killer instinct" might seem paradoxical, yet it perfectly encapsulates the essence of Pogačar's competitive nature. His happiness is genuine, stemming from a love for the sport and the joy of pushing human limits, but this joy does not soften his resolve. Instead, it fuels an inner fire that propels him to seek excellence every single day. His smile is not a mask; it's a testament to how he channels passion and intensity into positive energy that enhances, rather than detracts from, his ability to compete at the highest level.

This duality has roots in his early years. Growing up in Slovenia, cycling was as much a joyful exploration as it was a challenge. The freedom of the open road, the thrill of racing through mountainous terrain, and the camaraderie of his teammates instilled a deep-seated love for the sport. From the outset, Pogačar approached competition with a lightness of spirit that kept pressure at bay and allowed him to perform without the crippling weight of fear or doubt. His natural exuberance on the bike made him stand out among peers, not just for his talent but for the way he embraced every moment with infectious enthusiasm.

Yet this joy was never mistaken for complacency. Behind the smiles, there was always a calculated intensity, a hunger that refused to be sated. Even in training, where the grind is often monotonous and punishing, he approached every session with a fierce dedication. His laughter on the outside contrasted with the steely focus that allowed him to push through pain and fatigue others might find unbearable. This combination gave him a psychological edge, as it demonstrated an ability to endure hardship without letting it consume his spirit.

Observers who have worked closely with Pogačar often remark on his unshakeable confidence, a quiet, self-assured belief that he is capable of extraordinary feats. This confidence is deeply intertwined with his joyful outlook. Rather than approaching races as battles to survive, he sees them as stages to express himself and his craft. This perspective transforms pressure into opportunity and anxiety into excitement. It is a mindset that allows him to smile in the face of adversity, knowing that every challenge is a chance to prove his mettle.

What makes his killer instinct so compelling is that it is never reckless or arrogant. Pogačar's hunger is disciplined and respectful. He understands the value of humility and the importance of respecting opponents. His smile often masks the intense mental calculation happening beneath the surface, where he weighs risks, studies rivals, and formulates plans. The joy he radiates coexists with a ruthless competitiveness that demands nothing less than total commitment.

This balance between joy and intensity manifests vividly during the heat of competition. When he crosses the finish line victorious, the elation on his face is unmistakable, pure, unfiltered joy that celebrates months of sacrifice and hours of relentless effort. But when the race is still unfolding, that same face can harden into fierce concentration, with eyes narrowing and muscles tightening, signaling that his killer instinct has taken over. He becomes a predator locked onto his target, moving with precision and intent that leaves little room for error.

One iconic moment that captures this duality occurred during the 2021 Tour de France. Throughout the race, Pogačar was known for his joyful interactions with fans and teammates, often seen smiling, joking, and even playfully teasing rivals. Yet when the decisive climbs arrived, his demeanor shifted subtly but unmistakably. His focus sharpened; the joy became a weapon, a source of energy that powered his attacks. The grin never disappeared entirely, but it was accompanied by a laser-like intensity that signaled he was in ruthless pursuit of victory.

This joyful killer instinct also protects him from the psychological pitfalls that plague many elite athletes. The pressure of expectations, media scrutiny, and self-imposed demands can erode confidence and lead to burnout. Pogačar's ability to maintain a positive, joyful mindset allows him to absorb and deflect these stresses. His smile is both a shield and a beacon, helping him stay grounded and connected to what first drew him to cycling, the pure pleasure of riding.

Behind closed doors, his competitive drive reveals itself in countless ways. Teammates describe him as a perfectionist who sets extremely high standards for himself. His relentless pursuit of marginal gains, whether in training, nutrition, or tactics, stems from an inner hunger that never wanes. The smiles and laughter often give way to quiet moments of intense reflection and analysis, where he scrutinizes every detail in search of improvement. This process is fueled not by fear of failure but by a desire to keep raising the bar, to continually evolve as a rider and competitor.

His hunger extends beyond personal achievement; it is also about legacy. Pogačar is acutely aware of the history of cycling and the legends who came before him. This awareness adds another layer of motivation. He doesn't just want to win races, he wants to etch his name among the greatest, to be remembered for a career that combined brilliance with heart. The joy he exudes thus carries the weight of ambition, driving him to chase records and push limits with the infectious enthusiasm that makes him beloved by fans and respected by rivals.

This vibrant inner fire also fuels his resilience. Cycling's grueling demands often bring physical and mental lows, but Pogačar's joyful killer instinct acts as a compass, guiding him through tough times. When faced with setbacks, injuries, or disappointments, his smile is a reminder of his deeper purpose and relentless will to return stronger. It's a smile that says, "I'm not done yet," a declaration of ongoing hunger and unyielding spirit.

The paradox of joy and ruthless competitiveness in Pogačar challenges common stereotypes about what it takes to succeed at the highest level of sport. He proves that ferocity does not require grimness, and that a genuine love for one's craft can coexist with a ruthless ambition to win. His smiling face belies the fierce determination inside, a rare combination that inspires and captivates those who witness his journey.

Tadej Pogačar's joyful killer instinct defines not just how he races but who he is. It is a dynamic force that drives him to extraordinary heights while keeping his humanity intact. This blend of lightness and intensity, warmth and steel, makes him a uniquely compelling figure in the world of cycling, a champion whose hunger never fades, whose smile never masks the fierce competitor within, but rather reveals the powerful joy of pursuing greatness.

Chapter 9
Off the Bike, Still a Champion

How fellow cyclist Urška Žigart became his anchor, teammate, and co-dreamer

Tadej Pogačar's story is often told through the lens of his breathtaking feats on two wheels, the blistering climbs, the strategic brilliance, the triumphant podium moments. Yet behind the scenes, away from the roar of the crowds and the flashing cameras, there is a deeply human story that has been quietly shaping the champion's life and career: the love and partnership he shares with Urška Žigart. Their relationship stands as a testament to how love, mutual respect, and shared dreams can anchor even the most whirlwind of careers, creating a foundation that nourishes success and fuels ambition.

Urška Žigart is no stranger to the world of professional cycling. Like Tadej, she has forged her own path in the demanding sport, carving out a reputation as a strong, determined rider in women's professional cycling. Their bond blossomed through a shared understanding of the sacrifices, struggles, and triumphs that come with life on the bike. They found in each other not just a partner, but a teammate in every sense of the word, someone who knows the language of cycling, the weight of expectations, and the highs and lows of racing. This connection, built on empathy and shared passion, would become one of the most important pillars in Pogačar's life.

Their story began like many romances: quietly, naturally, with a friendship that deepened as they navigated the unique challenges of pro cycling life together. Training camps, long rides through the Slovenian countryside, and the grinding schedule of races created a rhythm that pulled them closer. Yet their relationship was never just about convenience or proximity. They recognized early on that their dreams aligned and their values matched, they were both committed to pushing boundaries and seeking greatness, not just for themselves but as a team.

For Tadej, Urška became a vital source of balance. The pressures of being one of the world's most celebrated cyclists could be overwhelming, but with her, he found solace and grounding. Their conversations weren't only about tactics or performance metrics; they talked about hopes, fears, the small joys of everyday life that often get lost in the shadow of professional demands. This emotional anchor gave Pogačar a sense of normalcy amid the chaos of international competition.

Urška's presence also challenged traditional ideas of support within the sport. While many elite athletes rely heavily on coaches, trainers, and sports psychologists, the emotional strength drawn from a loving partner who truly understands the athlete's world is a profound advantage. Their relationship exemplifies how personal connections can enhance professional performance, the quiet encouragement, the shared understanding of pain and perseverance, the celebrations of victories both big and small.

As their partnership grew, so too did their shared vision. They became co-dreamers, not just supporting each other's individual goals but imagining a future where they could celebrate collective success. The idea of two athletes, equally passionate and driven, pushing one another toward excellence brought a powerful dynamic. This mutual motivation was not competitive in a destructive sense but rather symbiotic, each inspired the other to reach higher, to train harder, and to remain resilient when faced with setbacks.

Urška's own career flourished alongside Tadej's meteoric rise, and their journeys often intertwined. They trained side by side, traveled together to races, and shared insights from their respective experiences on the men's and women's circuits. This partnership brought a richness to both of their careers, as they learned from each other's strengths and perspectives. It was a rare example of a relationship where personal and professional lives intertwined seamlessly, each feeding the other.

One of the most striking aspects of their bond is how it humanizes the often glamorous and distant world of professional cycling. Pogačar is sometimes seen through the lens of his record-breaking achievements and public persona, but with Urška, he reveals a more vulnerable, authentic side. She is a confidante who has witnessed the long hours of struggle, the moments of doubt, and the personal sacrifices required to stay at the top. Her unwavering belief in him acts as a powerful antidote to the loneliness that can accompany elite competition.

Their love story is also one of mutual respect for the individuality and independence that each brings to the relationship. Despite their closeness, they maintain their identities as athletes first, with their own ambitions and challenges. This respect for autonomy fosters a healthy partnership where support does not mean losing oneself, but rather empowering each other to grow fully. It is a relationship built on trust, communication, and an understanding that both individuals bring unique strengths to the table.

In moments of crisis or pressure, this connection has proven to be a critical source of resilience for Pogačar. The grueling demands of the sport, the expectations of millions, and the physical toll of racing could easily overwhelm. Yet knowing that Urška stands beside him, not just as a cheerleader but as a teammate who intimately understands the journey, gives him emotional strength to face whatever comes. Their shared experiences create a bond that transcends the sport, a partnership forged in mutual endurance and celebration.

Their love also serves as a beacon for younger athletes and fans, illustrating that even at the highest echelons of competitive sport, personal relationships matter deeply. The story of Pogačar and Žigart challenges the myth of the solitary athlete, instead highlighting the importance of connection, balance, and emotional well-being. It shows that behind every champion is often a network of support and love that sustains them through the highs and lows.

The couple's public appearances and social media interactions reveal a warmth and playfulness that endears them to fans worldwide. Their chemistry is evident in shared smiles, gentle teasing, and the subtle ways they support each other in public forums. These glimpses into their private world break down barriers between athlete and audience, making the extraordinary achievements feel accessible and deeply human.

Looking ahead, their relationship promises to be a continuing source of strength and inspiration. As both pursue the ever-changing challenges of professional cycling, their partnership will no doubt adapt and evolve. But the core, a foundation built on shared passion, unwavering support, and co-dreaming of greatness, remains steadfast. This love story is not just a footnote in Pogačar's career; it is a central chapter that helps explain the resilience, balance, and hunger that define the man behind the victories.

The narrative of Tadej Pogačar and Urška Žigart is about more than just two cyclists who fell in love. It is about how human connection fuels ambition, how partnership can become a wellspring of strength, and how love can be the quiet force that enables extraordinary achievement. Their journey together reminds us that even in a world measured by seconds and kilometers, the heart remains the greatest engine of all.

Despite fame and fortune, he still prefers home-cooked meals and Slovenian forests

Tadej Pogačar's journey from the quiet villages of Slovenia to the brightest stages of professional cycling has brought him a level of fame and fortune that few athletes ever experience. Yet, despite his global renown and the millions that have flowed in through prize money, endorsements, and sponsorship deals, his lifestyle remains grounded in a remarkable sense of modesty and simplicity. This contrast between his superstar status and his humble personal habits forms a key part of what makes him so compelling, not just as a champion on the bike, but as a person who never lets success disconnect him from his roots.

While the world around him often buzzes with the glitz and glamour of celebrity culture, Pogačar finds his sanctuary away from the public eye in the unassuming comforts of home. Instead of succumbing to the temptation of extravagant living, he cherishes the familiar embrace of home-cooked meals and the peaceful solitude of Slovenia's forests. This preference reflects a deeply held belief that true richness lies not in material excess but in authenticity and connection to one's origins.

The Slovenian countryside, with its rolling hills, dense woods, and serene trails, has long been more than just a backdrop for his training rides, it's a source of emotional refuge and inspiration. After intense days filled with the pressure and intensity of professional racing, returning to these natural spaces offers Pogačar a chance to recharge both body and mind. The forests are not just scenic spots; they represent continuity, a living link to the boy he was before fame transformed his life.

In a world where athletes often surround themselves with luxury cars, opulent mansions, and designer everything, Pogačar's home remains a place of understated warmth and comfort. Family and tradition take center stage there, shaping the atmosphere with familiar scents of Slovenian cooking, fresh vegetables, hearty stews, homemade breads, and dishes that carry the flavors of his childhood. This connection to food is more than nourishment; it's a celebration of culture and identity that keeps him rooted.

Pogačar's commitment to home-cooked meals signals his broader approach to life, thoughtful, intentional, and deeply respectful of simplicity. He knows that fueling a champion's body demands discipline and care, but that doesn't mean sacrificing pleasure or the intimacy of shared meals. The act of sitting down with loved ones to enjoy food prepared with care offers him a rare kind of joy and grounding amid the demands of his high-profile career.

This modest lifestyle is also a reflection of his character, humble, approachable, and unpretentious. Teammates and those close to him often describe Pogačar as someone who doesn't let success inflate his ego or create distance. Instead, he remains accessible and genuine, qualities that make him beloved by fans and respected within the cycling community. His modesty invites connection rather than alienation, reminding everyone that greatness need not come at the cost of humility.

The simplicity he embraces outside the professional realm can also be seen as a strategic choice. The whirlwind of fame and expectation that accompanies a superstar cyclist could easily become overwhelming or distracting. By maintaining a lifestyle that prioritizes familiar comforts, Pogačar builds a protective buffer against the chaos. This balance allows him to navigate the complexities of elite sport without losing sight of who he is beneath the accolades and public attention.

His affinity for Slovenian forests is not just sentimental, it also ties directly into his mental and physical well-being. Nature walks, hikes, and quiet moments surrounded by trees serve as a form of therapy, helping to clear his mind and relieve stress. This relationship with the outdoors nurtures resilience, providing a space where worries dissipate and focus sharpens. It's a vital counterpoint to the high stakes and high speeds of his racing calendar.

Despite the millions at his disposal, Pogačar does not seek the limelight outside the racecourse. He avoids flashy displays of wealth or status symbols that could alienate him from the ordinary people who have supported his journey since the beginning. This restraint underscores a grounded worldview shaped by his upbringing and the values instilled by his family. Money, while enabling certain comforts and opportunities, has not altered his fundamental sense of self or his priorities.

In conversations with journalists, Pogačar often expresses gratitude for the simple pleasures of life, quiet mornings, good food, time spent outdoors, and the company of close friends and family. These moments, seemingly small, form the foundation of his happiness and resilience. They are reminders that no matter how far his career takes him, the core of who he is remains unchanged.

This modesty does not imply a lack of ambition or drive. Rather, it reveals a maturity and self-awareness that are rare among athletes who reach his level of success. He understands that true strength comes from balance, the ability to pursue greatness while nurturing one's humanity. The choice to embrace a grounded lifestyle is an extension of the same discipline and clarity that guide him on the bike.

His reluctance to indulge in extravagant habits has also influenced how he manages his public image and personal brand. Unlike many celebrities who craft highly curated personas, Pogačar's authenticity resonates powerfully with fans. They see in him not just a champion, but a relatable figure whose achievements feel attainable because they are anchored in real life and real values.

Behind the scenes, this modest lifestyle fosters a work ethic and mental clarity that translate into performance gains. Without the distractions of excessive luxury or the pressure to maintain a glamorous facade, Pogačar can focus fully on training, recovery, and preparation. The comfort of home-cooked meals provides consistent, wholesome nutrition that supports his demanding physical regimen, while the tranquility of natural surroundings helps maintain mental sharpness.

His story is a reminder that in the high-pressure world of elite sports, humility and simplicity can be powerful assets. Pogačar's example challenges the narrative that success must lead to excess, showing instead that staying connected to one's roots and embracing modest pleasures can cultivate the strength needed to excel.

The image of Tadej Pogačar sitting down at a wooden table, sharing a meal made with love, surrounded by the quiet beauty of the Slovenian landscape, speaks volumes about the man behind the victories. It is a portrait of a champion who has found a way to thrive without losing himself, a rare blend of extraordinary talent and profound humility.

107

This connection to home and tradition also fuels his passion for cycling itself. The sport is not just a career but a lifelong pursuit intertwined with memories of childhood rides and the beauty of his homeland. Every race, every pedal stroke carries the echo of those early experiences, grounding his success in a narrative much larger than medals or money.

In an era where fame often distances athletes from their origins, Pogačar's modesty stands as a beacon of authenticity. His story offers inspiration not only to aspiring cyclists but to anyone striving to maintain balance amid the pressures of modern life. It shows that no matter how high one rises, the true measure of success may lie in the ability to stay humble, cherish the simple things, and remember where you come from.

His growing philanthropic efforts and belief in cycling as a force for good

Tadej Pogačar's impact stretches far beyond his astonishing achievements on the racecourse. As his career soared, so did his awareness of the platform he had gained, and the responsibility that came with it. His commitment to giving back has grown steadily, evolving from personal acts of kindness into more organized philanthropic efforts. For Pogačar, cycling is not just a sport or a career; it is a powerful vehicle to inspire positive change, foster community, and open doors for others. His belief that the bicycle can be a force for good permeates every charitable initiative he supports, reflecting a deep conviction that success must be shared and multiplied.

From the earliest days of his rise, Pogačar's humility and generosity were evident. Whether in small hometown gestures or supporting local causes, he has never forgotten the people and places that shaped him. This grounded approach allowed him to build genuine connections with fans and communities who often see him as more than just a champion. It was clear that his victories were not solely personal triumphs but celebrations shared with those around him.

As his profile expanded on the international stage, so did his capacity to influence and mobilize resources. His philanthropic focus ranges widely, from grassroots cycling programs that nurture young talent to environmental causes promoting sustainability and clean living. One of the most significant aspects of his giving is the emphasis on accessibility and inclusion, ensuring cycling's benefits reach people regardless of background, age, or ability.

The foundations of his philanthropic philosophy lie in his belief that cycling offers far more than physical exercise. It embodies freedom, empowerment, and a connection to nature that has the power to uplift individuals and communities alike. Whether it's helping children discover the joy of riding or advocating for safer cycling infrastructure, Pogačar's efforts echo this transformative potential.

Among his key initiatives is support for youth development programs in Slovenia and other cycling communities across Europe. These projects focus on breaking down barriers to participation by providing bikes, coaching, and safe spaces to ride. Many young riders from economically challenged backgrounds have found a path forward through these programs, sometimes even glimpsing a future in competitive cycling thanks to the doors Pogačar's involvement helps open. His commitment to nurturing the next generation underscores a sense of responsibility to pass forward the opportunities he was fortunate to receive.

Moreover, his outreach extends into health and wellness initiatives where cycling plays a therapeutic role. Collaborations with organizations addressing mental health highlight his understanding of the holistic benefits of sport. Pogačar's own experience of maintaining balance through outdoor activity adds authenticity to these efforts. He recognizes the power of movement and nature to heal and sustain, making his support for such causes deeply personal.

Environmental stewardship is another pillar of his philanthropic work. The simplicity of a bicycle aligns perfectly with sustainable living, and Pogačar champions this message passionately. Campaigns promoting cycling as an eco-friendly alternative to motorized transport align with his values of preserving the natural landscapes he cherishes. This commitment has translated into partnerships with environmental groups and public awareness drives, encouraging fans and communities to adopt greener lifestyles. His voice adds weight to the growing global conversation about climate change and the urgent need for action.

Pogačar's philanthropic activities also embrace charity rides and events designed to raise funds and awareness. These occasions bring together fans, fellow athletes, and communities in celebrations of shared purpose. Whether participating personally or lending his name and influence, Pogačar helps draw attention to causes ranging from education to social inclusion. These rides often create powerful moments of solidarity, where the joy of cycling intersects with the profound satisfaction of helping others.

His involvement with international cycling charities broadens his reach even further. By aligning with organizations working to develop cycling infrastructure in under-resourced areas, Pogačar contributes to building safer, healthier environments. These projects emphasize the role of cycling in fostering mobility, independence, and economic opportunity, particularly in regions where transportation options are limited. His global outlook on philanthropy demonstrates an awareness of cycling's universal value.

A remarkable dimension of Pogačar's giving lies in how he leverages his personal story to inspire change. His rise from modest beginnings to cycling superstardom serves as a beacon for young people around the world. He frequently uses interviews and social media to highlight charitable initiatives, encouraging fans to get involved and recognize their own capacity to make a difference. His authenticity and approachability amplify these messages, making philanthropy feel accessible rather than distant or abstract.

Behind the scenes, those who work with him on philanthropic projects emphasize his genuine interest and hands-on approach. Despite his demanding schedule, Pogačar dedicates time to meet with beneficiaries, visit project sites, and engage directly with communities. This personal involvement strengthens the impact of his efforts, reinforcing that his philanthropy is not simply about giving money but about building relationships and lasting change.

The values reflected in his charitable work echo the core principles that define Pogačar as an athlete, discipline, perseverance, and a focus on collective success. He often speaks about the importance of teamwork and support in cycling, concepts that translate seamlessly into his philanthropic vision. Recognizing that no victory is achieved in isolation, he extends this ethos outward to the broader communities who share his journey.

Cycling's global popularity has given Pogačar a platform unlike any other, and his use of this platform for social good sets him apart. While many athletes engage in charity, his efforts stand out for their coherence and alignment with his personal narrative. This integration makes his giving not just an add-on but an intrinsic part of who he is.

Fans frequently express admiration not just for his racing prowess but for the heart he shows off the bike. Stories circulate of Pogačar quietly donating bikes to children, sponsoring local clubs, or supporting causes with no fanfare. These acts reinforce a consistent image of a champion who sees success as a shared journey, not a solitary destination.

His belief in cycling as a force for good is a throughline connecting all his philanthropic work. Whether by fostering youth programs, promoting health, protecting the environment, or rallying communities around charitable events, Pogačar channels the power of the bike into meaningful social impact. This vision enriches the sport's legacy and offers a blueprint for how athletes can harness their influence responsibly.

Looking forward, Pogačar's philanthropic ambitions show no sign of waning. As his career continues, he plans to expand existing initiatives and explore new areas where cycling can drive positive change. The challenge of balancing elite competition with a growing role as a humanitarian inspires him, fueling a sense of purpose beyond personal glory.

His story of giving back resonates deeply with those who understand that true greatness transcends trophies and records. By using pedals and passion as tools for transformation, Pogačar has carved a place not only in cycling history but in the hearts of communities worldwide. His journey demonstrates that the impact of a champion extends far beyond the finish line, touching lives, inspiring hope, and building a better future on two wheels.

Chapter 10
Writing His Own Legend

A look at the unbroken records, unclaimed goals, and historic possibilities still ahead

The cycling world has long been captivated by the meteoric rise of Tadej Pogačar, a rider whose talent, determination, and character have set him apart from the pack. Yet even as he racks up an extraordinary list of victories and accolades, the question remains: what more can he win? This question is not just about tallying trophies; it probes the horizon of possibilities for a cyclist who has already rewritten history in multiple ways. The record books are filled with names and numbers, but Pogačar stands at the threshold of an era where new benchmarks await, and unclaimed goals beckon him toward unprecedented heights.

From the outset of his career, Pogačar's trajectory suggested something extraordinary. Few athletes have entered the sport with such an immediate impact, much less sustained excellence. With multiple Tour de France titles, triumphs in prestigious one-day classics, and a rare Triple Crown, he has already secured a place among cycling's elite. Yet his youth implies many seasons still lie ahead, offering fertile ground for new chapters and fresh milestones that could redefine greatness in the sport.

One of the most tantalizing prospects lies in the pursuit of longevity at the very pinnacle. Historically, the greatest cyclists who dominated the Grand Tours often saw their careers segmented into peaks and valleys, with some early brilliance followed by decline or injury. Pogačar's combination of youth, resilience, and a modern approach to training and recovery gives him a strong foundation to challenge these patterns. Should he maintain his health and motivation, the prospect of contending, and winning, Grand Tours well into his thirties opens the door to record-setting career totals that few can approach.

The record for most Tour de France wins is a hallowed benchmark in the sport, famously held by legends who have become household names. Pogačar has already matched the early trajectory of some of these icons. The possibility of surpassing this record looms large, not as mere speculation but as an achievable target if he continues on his current path. His ability to balance climbing prowess with time-trialling strength and tactical savvy has given him a rare versatility that could sustain dominance across diverse courses and evolving race dynamics. The Tour's physical and psychological demands are notorious, but Pogačar has demonstrated an uncanny capacity to handle pressure and adapt, qualities essential for such a historic run.

Beyond the Tour de France, the other Grand Tours, the Giro d'Italia and Vuelta a España, also present compelling arenas for Pogačar's ambitions. Already victorious in the Giro, his mastery of multi-week stage races reveals a capacity to excel across various terrains and race cultures. The challenge of conquering all three Grand Tours in a career, or even within a condensed period, is a feat that has eluded many greats. For Pogačar, the strategic targeting of these events, combined with his natural talent, creates the possibility of joining an exclusive club of riders who have mastered cycling's grandest stages comprehensively.

His dominance is not limited to stage races alone. The Classics, particularly the Monuments, are a different test, one that blends brute strength, tactical insight, and often the unpredictable chaos of one-day battles over challenging terrain. Pogačar has already taken iconic races like Strade Bianche, Tour of Flanders, and Il Lombardia. Each victory not only solidified his versatility but also raised questions about how many more such victories he might claim. Winning multiple editions of these monuments would place him alongside the sport's greatest specialists, carving out a dual legacy as both a Grand Tour general and a Classics master. The unique demands of these races mean that sustained success here requires a rider to reinvent and refine their skills continuously, a challenge Pogačar appears ready to embrace.

The world championships represent another rare and coveted prize that could further embellish Pogačar's palmarès. Wearing the rainbow jersey is a symbol of ultimate supremacy, and the chance to claim it multiple times remains an open door. His combination of endurance, speed, and race craft fits the profile of a rider who could excel in the varied courses the championship presents year after year. Given the intensity of the competition and the prestige of the title, each attempt offers both a test and an opportunity to demonstrate his ability to peak at the right moment under immense pressure.

There are also subtler, less tangible victories that could define Pogačar's legacy, those relating to the evolution of cycling itself. His riding style, blending raw power with refined technique and strategic intelligence, pushes the boundaries of what modern cyclists can achieve. Records in average speed, stage winning margins, and time-trial performance may all fall under his relentless pursuit of excellence. Advances in technology and training methodologies continue to open new frontiers, and Pogačar's openness to innovation suggests he will be at the forefront of cycling's future breakthroughs.

Pogačar's unclaimed goals also include historic 'firsts' that transcend personal achievement. Becoming the first Slovenian to secure multiple consecutive Tours or the first rider to complete a specific sequence of victories in a single season would solidify his national legacy while carving new spaces in the global narrative. His role as an ambassador for Slovenian cycling elevates these accomplishments beyond sport, inspiring generations and fueling a cycling renaissance in his home country.

The mental aspect of these ambitions cannot be overlooked. Pogačar's remarkable composure and humility in the face of escalating expectations signal a mindset well-suited for continued success. The hunger that has driven him since his earliest victories burns as brightly as ever, even as the pressures of fame and competition mount. This internal fire is a critical ingredient in achieving what many regard as impossible, allowing him to transform challenges and setbacks into fuel for growth.

Team dynamics and support structures will also influence what more he can achieve. Cycling is uniquely dependent on the collective strength of teammates, coaches, and support staff, and Pogačar has shown an ability to cultivate winning environments around him. His relationships with key teammates and staff foster cohesion and resilience that can turn tight races in his favor. Continued collaboration and adaptation in this arena will be pivotal as rivals emerge and race tactics evolve.

Looking beyond victories and records, the impact Pogačar has on the sport's culture and future generations may prove equally significant. As a figure who combines extraordinary talent with grace and approachability, he embodies a new kind of champion, one who inspires not just by winning but by his manner and values. His example encourages young riders to dream bigger, work harder, and maintain balance. This cultural legacy, though less measurable, could outlast even the most dazzling palmarès.

While the physical challenges of cycling will always be daunting, Pogačar's approach suggests a calculated balance of ambition and sustainability. He is aware that greatness demands preservation of body and mind over time. His training regimes and lifestyle choices reflect a long-term vision, aiming not only to win races but to remain a force for years to come. This strategic outlook, paired with his natural gifts, positions him to rewrite not just records but the very expectations of what a cycling career can encompass.

Cycling history is littered with legends who dazzled briefly or burned out under pressure. What sets Pogačar apart is a rare fusion of precocity and maturity, talent and temperament. These qualities hint at a career that could span multiple decades, filled with milestones that progressively raise the bar. Fans and experts alike watch with anticipation as each season unfolds, wondering which record he might shatter next or which new challenge he will embrace.

The road ahead is filled with uncertainties, racing is unpredictable, and even the greatest athletes face injuries, tactical surprises, and shifting competition. Yet Pogačar's story thus far has been one of overcoming obstacles and seizing opportunities with relentless focus. His journey offers a compelling narrative of what happens when raw ability meets unyielding dedication and an unshakeable belief in what is possible.

As he continues to write his own legend, the unbroken records, unclaimed goals, and historic possibilities stand as both milestones and motivators. Each victory adds a chapter, but the unfinished pages hold the greatest promise, inviting the world to witness what comes next from a rider who has already changed the sport forever.

What more can he win? The answer lies not only in trophies and titles but in the enduring mark he will leave on cycling's story, inspiring those who follow to chase their own extraordinary dreams.

Why even legends like Merckx, Hinault, and Contador speak of him in awed tones

There's a quiet gravity to the way cycling's most storied names speak about Tadej Pogačar. When legends like Eddy Merckx, Bernard Hinault, and Alberto Contador speak of a modern rider with reverence, it means something. These are not men easily impressed. Their careers were built on dominance, daring, and a relentless pursuit of greatness. For them to place a young Slovenian's name alongside their own is not casual praise, it's an acknowledgment that something rare is unfolding before their eyes.

Eddy Merckx, whose very name is synonymous with total cycling supremacy, has long been a benchmark for excellence. Known as "The Cannibal" for his insatiable appetite for victories, Merckx dominated every kind of race with an almost cruel efficiency. To hear him speak of Pogačar with admiration is startling and stirring. He has called Tadej one of the most complete riders he's ever seen, words that carry the weight of a man who has seen the evolution of the sport over decades. Merckx does not praise lightly. His career spanned 525 professional wins, and he has watched generations of riders try to emulate his model, most falling short. In Pogačar, he sees a kindred spirit: a cyclist who doesn't just win, but wins with style, with bravery, and with a joy that feels infectious.

Bernard Hinault's voice is more forceful, less sentimental. He ruled his era with fury, both respected and feared. Hinault won Grand Tours with aggression and a kind of uncompromising fire. He's spoken about Pogačar as a rider who respects the sport, but more importantly, as one who "attacks when he doesn't have to." That kind of boldness resonates with someone like Hinault. He recognizes in Pogačar a refusal to ride defensively, a distaste for passivity. That audacity is what makes champions unforgettable. It's what makes people watch, because they know something unexpected could happen at any moment. That kind of unpredictability is what kept Hinault on the front page for a decade. To him, Pogačar is more than a great rider. He's a showman with the legs to back it up.

Alberto Contador, more of a tactician and artist on the bike, has studied Pogačar's racing style with fascination. Contador, himself a winner of all three Grand Tours, is deeply analytical about what separates good from great. His respect for Pogačar is rooted in the younger rider's ability to suffer silently, to hold his cards until the precise moment, and then strike with ruthless precision. He's described watching Pogačar as "watching someone dance through pain." That's not just physical toughness, it's psychological control at its finest. Contador knows what it means to win when the world is watching and expecting, when every rival has marked your wheel and is waiting to exploit the smallest mistake. That Pogačar continues to win under that pressure convinces Contador that the Slovenian belongs in the pantheon already.

The awe these icons express is not born of sentimentality or nostalgia. It's grounded in an understanding of how brutal the sport is, how rare true dominance becomes in an era when marginal gains, data science, and team strategy often flatten individual flair. What Pogačar has managed to do, time and again, is transcend that flatness. He turns races into narratives again. He forces pundits to re-write expectations. The same sport that seemed to be dictated by spreadsheets and wattage suddenly feels wild, poetic, and unpredictable because of his presence.

What separates Pogačar's legacy-in-motion from so many others is his refusal to be boxed in. He isn't just a Tour specialist. He isn't just a climber. He isn't just a time trialist. He isn't just a Classics guy. He is all of them. The sheer breadth of his skillset brings to mind Merckx in the way he can line up at almost any kind of race and be the favorite. That kind of versatility used to define cycling's greatest legends, but in recent decades, as the sport became more specialized, it became less common. Watching Pogačar win on the brutal cobbles of Flanders, then climb with the best in the Alps, then solo to victory in San Remo or conquer gravel in Strade Bianche, is to watch a once-in-a-generation athlete restoring a lost art.

Even more astonishing is how he does it, with grace and humility that feel almost dissonant with his competitive intensity. That paradox, the gentle killer, has endeared him to fans and added to the legend. You can have all the victories in the world, but if the manner in which you race doesn't move people, your legacy will always be incomplete. Pogačar's charisma is not loud, not boastful. It's in the way he speaks with deference about his rivals. It's in the way he gives credit to his team even after soloing to glory. It's in his willingness to fail while trying something bold, rather than sitting safely in the bunch. That spirit has captivated the old guard because they know how hard it is to sustain that courage once the weight of expectation becomes constant.

For Merckx, who raced with a merciless hunger but also understood how lonely dominance could be, Pogačar seems like a rider who's figured out how to win without becoming closed off. For Hinault, whose own confrontations with the press and peloton were legendary, Pogačar's open demeanor is refreshing yet still anchored in steely resolve. For Contador, who agonized over tactics and form and timing, Pogačar seems to make it all look deceptively easy, an illusion that only the truly great can create.

Even riders outside the immediate cycling world have taken notice. Track cyclists, sprinters, mountain bikers, triathletes, many of them talk about Pogačar not just as an icon of road racing but as an athlete whose ethic transcends discipline. His commitment to training, his balance in life, and his emotional maturity despite youth make him a compelling role model in a sporting age often defined by burnout and ego. It's rare to find someone who loves the game this much and yet plays it so well.

When journalists ask the greats if Pogačar is already one of the best ever, the answer often comes with a smile: "Of course he is." There is no need to wait for retirement, no need to count every win. Legacy is not only about statistics. It's about impact. It's about changing how the sport is viewed, how it's raced, how it's loved. And by that measure, Pogačar is already towering among the giants. The fact that his story is still unfolding only makes the reverence deeper, because every race might offer another glimpse of magic.

That's what the legends see. Not just a rider. A movement. A moment. A force that calls back to the golden age of cycling, even as he forges a new path for its future. That's why their voices soften when they say his name. Because they know they're watching history in real time. Because they know what greatness looks like. And they see it now, in motion, in yellow, in rainbow, in mud-splattered white. They see it, and they remember.

Not just a cyclist, but a symbol of fearlessness, fun, and forever chasing what's next

Tadej Pogačar rides with a spark most can't fake and few can sustain. Watch him pedal through the Alps, across the gravel-strewn white roads of Tuscany, or up the jagged ramps of the Basque Country, and you see a man unshackled. What's most striking is not just the smoothness of his cadence or the precision of his attacks. It's the joy. The audacity. The fire in his eyes that says he's not just racing to win, but because something in his soul needs to feel the rawness of the chase. He has become far more than just a dominant cyclist, he is a symbol of what sport looks like when passion, talent, and fearlessness meet total freedom.

It's rare that someone so statistically dominant also radiates the kind of emotional pull that Pogačar does. On paper, he is a generational force. Two Tour de France wins before age 24. Monuments claimed in solo style. A Giro conquered. Rainbow stripes secured. But what elevates him is that he refuses to become mechanical in pursuit of greatness. While rivals dissect data, Pogačar seems to dance. He improvises. He races with feel. And when he throws down an attack, it often feels like it was born not from spreadsheets but from instinct, something untamed and thrilling that can't quite be taught.

Even his defeats have shaped him without dimming his light. When Jonas Vingegaard struck him down in 2022 and again in 2023, many wondered whether the Slovenian's wings had been clipped. But Pogačar never flinched from the pain. He absorbed it. He studied it. Then he returned, not just stronger, but brighter. His 2024 season was proof that he hadn't shrunk from the fire, but had stepped deeper into it. He didn't merely want revenge; he wanted to evolve. To remind people that cycling is not only about marginal gains and cautious calculation, but also about brave hearts willing to race on feel. That's what he did. That's who he is.

Talk to his competitors and you'll hear a mix of frustration and admiration. They can't predict him. They can't contain him. And that unpredictability is terrifying because it's tethered to real strength, not just flair. Riders know he might attack with 80 kilometers to go, because he has. They know he might grin mid-race or wave to a child holding a Slovenian flag, because he does. And they also know that when he does those things, he's probably still going to drop them on the next climb.

His mystique isn't cultivated. It's real. It flows from the way he talks about the bike like it's an old friend, not a tool. From the way he shrugs off expectations in interviews, often laughing them away, and from how he never seems burdened by the weight of his own greatness. He carries it lightly, like someone who understands how fleeting this moment could be, and chooses to squeeze every drop of wonder from it. There's a boyish quality to his spirit, one that hasn't been worn down by contracts or critics. And yet, underneath that lightness, there's a competitive steel forged in solitude, loss, and effort no one else sees.

Pogačar's relationship with pain is different from most. He doesn't grimace or scowl his way up mountain passes. He leans into the suffering with serenity. It's not that it doesn't hurt, it's that he seems to know how to make peace with the agony and ride through it with clarity. That kind of mindset can't be manufactured. It comes from a place deep inside, where self-belief and purpose collide. Where failure is never final. Where doubt exists, but never dictates.

And yet, for all his brilliance, Pogačar has never stopped being deeply, visibly human. He gives honest post-race interviews, not rehearsed lines. He takes losses on the chin. He claps for others. He tweets with mischief and humility. He celebrates birthdays with cake and without fanfare. He'll ride a children's bike in a parking lot or joke around in training camp with teammates. That ability to remain grounded while achieving almost unthinkable things is part of why his legend feels so lived-in already. He's not performing for cameras. He's living his truth. And people feel it.

His personality bleeds into the way he races. Fearlessness is not just about attacking early or descending fast. It's about being willing to fail gloriously rather than fade away safely. That's what Pogačar brings. That's what fans crave in an age where sports can feel choreographed and sanitized. He injects chaos into a system obsessed with order. And somehow, more often than not, he emerges from that chaos triumphant. Because he isn't afraid of it. He welcomes it.

The future, for Pogačar, isn't just about how many jerseys he can hang in his closet. It's about how far he can stretch the possibilities of what one rider can do. Could he win all five Monuments? He's already two down. Could he double his Tour count? Maybe. Could he target Olympic gold, time trials, new formats, or even cyclocross or gravel? It's impossible to say what he won't try. Because he doesn't limit himself. He doesn't race with fear of losing. He races with curiosity. With fire. With freedom.

What that creates is a kind of emotional gravity. People are drawn to him not only because he wins, but because he feels alive every time he clips in. That aliveness resonates with those who know how hard it is to stay joyful in a world that demands results. He's become a mirror for the best parts of sport, playfulness, courage, and a refusal to be boxed into what's expected.

It's no wonder that young cyclists idolize him, that fans from countries far removed from cycling culture wear his jersey, that race directors hope he lines up. Because when he races, the world pays attention. And not just to the scoreboard. To the spirit of the thing. To the way he grabs a race by the throat, or the way he throws a bottle to a kid on the roadside, or the way he softens the shoulders of a teammate with a kind word after a brutal day.

Tadej Pogačar is not a myth being built in retrospect. He is a living, breathing flame, one you can feel every time he dares to make a move that shouldn't work, but somehow does. One you can sense in the grin he flashes after a victory, or even a defeat. Because both matter to him. Both teach. Both burn.

He is defined by fire, not just the kind that comes from effort, but the kind that comes from intention. And he is defined by freedom, not the absence of structure, but the presence of choice. He chooses to chase, to risk, to trust his gut. And he chooses, always, to love the bike.

What makes him a legend in motion is not just what he's won. It's what he represents: a fearless dreamer with legs of steel and a heart wide open to whatever comes next. That's the kind of figure sport rarely sees. And when it does, it never forgets.

CONCLUSION

Some athletes rewrite record books. A rarer few rewrite the emotional blueprint of a sport. Tadej Pogačar has done both. Watching his journey unfold has been like witnessing a painter rediscovering color, or a musician writing symphonies in a genre that didn't exist before. His brilliance stretches beyond the steep gradients, the solo breakaways, the Grand Tour podiums. It lives in the questions he makes people ask: What if the sport could be raced differently? What if victory could come with a smile, not just a grimace? What if the purest form of dominance wasn't brute force, but joy-infused boldness?

His career is still very much in motion, yet the story so far reads like a legend in fast-forward. He has crashed, soared, suffered, laughed, and stunned. But none of it feels rehearsed. That's what gives his narrative such rare texture. There's spontaneity in the way he competes, a refusal to let the burden of expectation weigh down his style. He does not ride for history books, though they follow him wherever he goes. He rides because something deep inside him still gets excited at the sight of a twisty descent or a silent mountain pass. That instinct, that unfiltered connection to the bike, has never left him.

What makes Pogačar different isn't just the scale of his achievements. It's the emotional honesty of his presence. Fans feel like they know him, even if they've never met him. Because he doesn't shield his humanity behind sunglasses or headlines. He wears it openly, in the way he reacts to defeat, in the way he celebrates with others, in the way he jokes when things go wrong. That humility, that authentic self-awareness, has allowed him to become not just a champion but a cultural touchstone for resilience and fearlessness.

His legacy, though still building, already stands as a challenge to the next generation: Don't just chase greatness, enjoy the ride. Innovate. Take risks. Make the mountains yours. Find the magic in your own rhythm. Because the path Pogačar rides is not paved with formulas; it's lit by intuition, heart, and a relentless curiosity to see how far he can stretch his limits.

And yet, for all the milestones he's passed, the most exhilarating part of his story is the sense that he's still chasing something. Not trophies. Not approval. But the feeling that comes when legs are screaming, crowds are roaring, and there's still one attack left in the tank. That moment, raw and fleeting, is his true finish line, always moving, always calling.

The world of cycling has long waited for a figure like this. Someone who could dominate without destroying the soul of the sport. Someone who could remind both fans and peers that courage still matters. That unpredictability still has a place. That the most powerful moves are sometimes the least expected.

Tadej Pogačar didn't just enter cycling's highest echelon. He redefined its ceiling. And no matter how far he climbs from here, one truth will remain: he's not racing to escape anything. He's racing to feel alive. And that's what makes him unforgettable.

Printed in Dunstable, United Kingdom

67157112R00077

ISBN 9798288190087

9 798288 190087